THE MAGIC FLUTE

OPERA JOURNEYS LIBRETTO SERIES

Wolfgang Amadeus Mozart's

THE MAGIC FLUTE

Complete Libretto
with Music Highlight examples

Edited by Burton D. Fisher
Principal lecturer, *Opera Journeys Lecture Series*

Opera Journeys Publishing™/Coral Gables, Florida

Copyright © 2001 by Opera Journeys Publishing

All rights reserved

No part of this publication may be reproduced, stored in a retrieval system, or transmitted, in any form or by any means, electronic, mechanical, photocopying, recording, or otherwise, without the prior permission of the authors.

All musical notations contained herein are original transcriptions by Opera Journeys Publishing.

Printed in the United States of America

WEB SITE: www.operajourneys.com E MAIL: operaj@bellsouth.net

Libretto

THE MAGIC FLUTE

ACT I - Scene 1	**Page 5**
ACT I - Scene 2	**Page 20**
ACT I - Scene 3	**Page 26**
ACT II - Scene 1	**Page 37**
ACT II - Scene 2	**Page 39**
ACT II - Scene 3	**Page 47**
ACT II - Scene 4	**Page 52**
ACT II - Scene 5	**Page 58**
ACT II - Scene 6	**Page 61**
ACT II - Scene 7	**Page 67**
ACT II - Scene 8	**Page 70**
ACT II - Scene 9	**Page 73**
ACT II - Scene 10	**Page 74**

ACT I - Scene 1

A rocky, rugged cliff setting. Tamino, dressed in hunting clothes, appears with a bow but no arrows. He is being pursued by a serpent.

TAMINO:
Zu Hülfe! Zu Hülfe! Sonst bin ich verloren,
der listigen Schlange zum Opfer erkoren.
Barmherzige Götter! Schon nahet sie sich!
Ach, rettet mich! Ach, schützet mich!

TAMINO:
Help! Help! Otherwise I'm lost, and I'll become a victim of the cunning serpent. Merciful Gods! It's already getting closer. Oh, save me! Oh, protect me!

*Exhausted, Tamino falls down and becomes unconscious.
Three veiled ladies appear, carrying silver darts.*

DREI DAMEN:
Stirb, Ungeheuer! Durch unsre Macht!

THE LADIES:
Die, you monster, our power will kill you!

(The Three Ladies kill the serpent.)

Triumph! Triumph! Sie ist vollbracht,
die Heldentat! Er ist befreit durch unsres
Armes Tapferkeit.

We did it! We did it! We accomplished an heroic deed! He has been saved by our courage.

ERSTE DAME:
Ein holder Jüngling, sanft und schön!

FIRST LADY: *(looking at Tamino)*
What a noble, gentle, handsome young man!

ZWEITE DAME:
So schön, als ich noch nie gesehn!

SECOND LADY:
I've never seen such a handsome man!

DRITTE DAME:
Ja, ja, gewiß zum Malen schön!

DREI DAMEN:
Würd' ich mein Herz der Liebe weihn,
so müßt es dieser Jüngling sein.
Laßt uns zu uns'rer Fürstin eilen,
ihr diese Nachricht zu erteilen.
Vielleicht daß dieser schöne Mann
die vor'ge Ruh' ihr geben kann.

ERSTE DAME:
So geht und sagt es ihr,
ich bleib indessen hier.

ZWEITE DAME:
Nein, nein, geht ihr nur hin,
ich wache hier für ihn!

DRITTE DAME:
Nein, nein, das kann nicht sein!
Ich schütze ihn allein.

ERSTE DAME:
Ich bleib' indessen hier!

ZWEITE DAME:
Ich wache hier für ihn!

DRITTE DAME:
Ich schütze ihn allein!

ERSTE DAME:
Ich bleibe!

ZWEITE DAME:
Ich wache!

DRITTE DAME:
Ich schütze!

DREI DAMEN:
Ich! Ich! Ich!
Ich sollte fort? Ei, ei, wie fein!
Sie wären gern bei ihm allein.
Nein, nein! Das kann nicht sein!

THIRD LADY:
He's handsome enough to be painted!

ALL:
If I would give my heart away
it would be to this young man.
Let's hurry to our Queen and tell her about
this news.
Maybe this handsome man can calm her
anxiety.

FIRST LADY:
So go and tell her. In the meantime I'm
staying here.

SECOND LADY:
No, no, you go,
I'll watch over him!

THIRD LADY:
No, no, that can't be! I'll protect him
myself.

FIRST LADY:
I'll stay here in the meantime!

SECOND LADY:
I'll watch over him!

THIRD LADY:
I'll protect him!

FIRST LADY:
I'll stay!

SECOND LADY:
I'll watch!

THIRD LADY:
I'll protect him!

THREE LADIES: *(each to themselves)*
I! I! I!
I should leave? Ha, ha, great!
She would love to be alone with him.
No, no! That can't be!

(each by themselves and then together)

Was wollte ich darum nicht geben,	What I wouldn't give if I could live with
könnt' ich mit diesem Jüngling leben!	this young man!
Hätt' ich ihn doch so ganz allein!	If I only I had him all to myself!
Doch keine geht; es kann nicht sein,	But that can't be, they're not leaving.
am besten ist es nun, ich geh'.	Therefore, it's best that I leave now.
	(to Tamino)
Du Jüngling, schön und liebevoll,	You handsome and lovable young man,
du trauter Jüngling, lebe wohl,	farewell till I see you again.
bis ich dich wiederseh'.	

The Three Ladies leave. Tamino awakens and looks around him fearfully.

TAMINO:
Wo bin ich? Ist's Fantasie, daß ich noch lebe? Oder hat eine höhere Macht mich gerettet?

Wie? Die bösartige Schlange ist tot?

Was hör ich? Ha, eine männliche Figur nähert sich.

TAMINO:
Where am I? Am I really still alive or did a higher power save me?

(He gets up and looks around)
What? That evil serpent is dead?

(The sound of a flute is heard in the distance.)
What do I hear? Oh, I see a man approaching.

Tamino hides behind a tree. Papageno arrives, dressed in feathers.
He carries a large bird cage on his back that is filled with various birds.
In his hands he holds a small flute.

Andante
PAPAGENO

Der Vo-gel-fän-ger bin ich ja, stets lu - stig hei - sa hop-sa-sa!

PAPAGENO:
Der Vogelfänger bin ich ja,
stets lustig, heisa, hopsasa!
Ich Vogelfänger bin bekannt
bei Alt und Jung im ganzen Land.
Weiß mit dem Locken umzugehn
und mich auf's Pfeifen zu verstehn.
Drum kann ich froh und lustig sein,
denn alle Vögel sind ja mein.

PAPAGENO:
I'm the bird-catcher, who's always happy!
Hi ho!
I'm known all over by young and old.
I know how to whistle every sound,
and I know all the birdcalls.
That's why I can be merry and happy,
because all the birds are mine.

Der Vogelfänger bin ich ja,	I'm the bird-catcher, who's always happy!
stets lustig, heisa, hopsassa!	Hi ho!
Ich Vogelfänger bin bekannt	I'm known all over by young and old.
bei Alt und Jung im ganzen Land.	
Ein Netz für Mädchen möchte ich,	I'd like to have a net to catch girls by the
ich fing sie dutzendweis für mich.	dozens.
Dann sperrte ich sie bei mir ein,	I would lock them safely at home so that
und alle Mädchen wären mein.	they'd all be mine.
Wenn alle Mädchen wären mein,	When they'd be mine, I'd give them sugar,
so tauschte ich brav Zucker ein.	but I'd give sugar right away to the one I
Die, welche mir am liebsten wär',	love most.
der gäb' ich gleich den Zucker her.	
Und küßte sie mich zärtlich dann,	Then if she would kiss me tenderly, it
wär' sie mein Weib und ich ihr Mann.	would be as if we were husband and wife.
Sie schlief' an meiner Seite ein,	She would sleep beside me, and I would
ich wiegte wie ein Kind sie ein.	rock her like a baby.

As Papageno blows his flute and begins to leave,
Tamino emerges from behind the tree where he was hiding.

TAMINO:
He da!

TAMINO:
Hey you!!

PAPAGENO:
Was da?

PAPAGENO:
What's that?

TAMINO:
Sag mir, du lustiger Freund, wer du seist?

TAMINO:
Tell me who you are, jolly friend?

PAPAGENO:
Wer ich bin? Dumme Frage!

Ein Mensch, wie du. Und wenn ich dich nun fragte, wer du bist?

PAPAGENO: *(to himself)*
Who I am? What a stupid question!
(aloud)
I'm a man just like you. And what if I asked you who you are?

TAMINO:
So würde ich dir antworten, daß ich aus fürstlichem Geblüte bin.

TAMINO:
I would answer you, that I come from royal ancestry.

PAPAGENO:
Das ist mir zu hoch. Mußt dich deutlicher erklären, wenn ich dich verstehen soll!

PAPAGENO:
That's too complicated. You have to explain that better in order for me to understand you.

THE MAGIC FLUTE

TAMINO:
Mein Vater ist ein Fürst, der über viele Länder und Menschen herrscht; darum nennt man mich Prinz.

PAPAGENO:
Länder? Menschen? Prinz? Sagst du mir zuvor: gibt's außer diesen Bergen auch noch Länder und Menschen?

TAMINO:
Viele Tausende!

PAPAGENO:
Da ließe sich ja eine Spekulation mit meinen Vögeln machen.

TAMINO:
Aber wie nennt man eigentlich diese Gegend? Und wer beherrscht sie?

PAPAGENO:
Das kann ich dir ebensowenig beantworten, als ich weiß, wie ich auf die Welt gekommen bin.

TAMINO:
Wie? Du wüßtest nicht, wo du geboren, oder wer deine Eltern waren?

PAPAGENO:
Kein Wort! Ich weiß nur so viel, daß nicht weit von hier meine Strohhütte steht, die mich vor Regen und Kälte schützt.

TAMINO:
Aber wie lebst du?

PAPAGENO:
Na, von Essen und Trinken, wie alle Menschen.

TAMINO:
Wodurch erhältst du das?

TAMINO:
My father is a king who rules many lands and peoples. That's why I'm called a prince.

PAPAGENO:
Many lands? People? Prince? Are you telling me that besides these mountains, other lands and peoples exist?

TAMINO:
Many thousands!

PAPAGENO:
My birds can figure that out.

TAMINO:
Tell me, what is this area called, and who rules it?

PAPAGENO:
I can't tell you that, just as I don't know how I came into this world.

TAMINO: *(laughs)*
What? You don't know where you were born and who your parents were?

PAPAGENO:
Quiet! I only know this much: that my straw cottage, which isn't far from here, protects me from the rain and cold.

TAMINO:
But how do you live?

PAPAGENO:
Just like everybody, from food and drink.

TAMINO:
How do you get that?

PAPAGENO:
Durch Tausch. Ich fange für die sternflammende Königin und ihre Jungfrauen verschiedene Vögel; dafür erhalte ich täglich Speise und Trank von ihr.

TAMINO:
Sternflammende Königin? Wenn es etwa gar die mächtige Herrscherin der Nacht wäre! Sag mir, guter Freund, warst du schon so glücklich, diese Göttin der Nacht zu sehen?

PAPAGENO:
Sehen? Die sternflammende Königin sehen? Welcher Sterbliche könnte sich rühmen, die je gesehn zu haben?

TAMINO:
Nun ist's klar; es ist eben diese nächtliche Königin, von der mein Vater mir so oft erzählte. Unfehlbar ist auch dieser Mann kein gewöhnlicher Mensch.

PAPAGENO:
Wie er mich so starr anblickt! Bald fang' ich an, mich vor ihm zu fürchten.

Warum siehst du so verdächtig und schelmisch nach mir?

TAMINO:
Weil... weil ich zweifle ob du ein Mensch bist.

PAPAGENO:
Wie war das?

TAMINO:
Nach deinen Federn, die dich bedecken, halt' ich dich...

PAPAGENO:
By trading. I catch various birds for the star-flaming Queen and her young ladies, and in exchange, I get my daily food and drink.

TAMINO:
Star-flaming Queen? If only she would be the almighty ruler of the night! Tell me, good friend, were you ever fortunate enough to see this goddess of the night?

PAPAGENO:
To see her? To see the star-flaming Queen? What earthly mortal could boast to have ever seen her?

TAMINO: *(to himself)*
Now I understand. It is this Queen of the Night that my father so often spoke to me about. Undoubtedly, this man also is no ordinary person.

PAPAGENO: *(to himself)*
How he stares at me! Soon I'll start to become afraid of him.
(aloud)
Why do you look at me so slyly and suspiciously?

TAMINO:
Because...because I doubt whether you're a real human being.

PAPAGENO:
What did you say?

TAMINO:
According to all those feathers covering you, I think you're...

(Tamino approaches Papageno)

PAPAGENO:
Doch für keinen Vogel? Du, bleib zurück, sag' ich, und traue mir nicht; denn ich habe Riesenkraft.

Wenn er sich nicht bald von mir schrecken lässt, so lauf ich davon.

TAMINO:
Riesenkraft?

Also warst du wohl gar mein Erretter, der diese giftige Schlange bekämpfte?

PAPAGENO:
Schlange!

Ah! Ah! Ist sie tot oder lebendig?

TAMINO:
Aber um alles in der Welt, Freund, wie hast du dieses Ungeheuer bekämpft? Du bist ohne Waffen.

PAPAGENO:
Brauch keine! Bei mir ist ein starker Druck mit der Hand mehr als Waffen.

TAMINO:
Du hast sie also erdrosselt?

PAPAGENO:
Erdrosselt!
Bin in meinem Leben nicht so stark gewesen, als heute.

PAPAGENO:
Not a bird, I hope? I'm telling you, stay back, and don't trust me, because I have gigantic strength.
(to himself)
If I don't scare him off soon, then I'll leave.

TAMINO:
Gigantic strength?
(He looks at the serpent.)
So it was you who rescued me by fighting this poisonous serpent?

PAPAGENO:
Serpent?
(He looks around and trembles)
Is it dead or alive?

TAMINO:
My friend, how on earth did you conquer this monster? You have no weapons!

PAPAGENO:
I don't need any! My strong hands are better than weapons.

TAMINO:
So you strangled it?

PAPAGENO:
Strangled! *(to himself)*
In my life, I've never been as strong as I am today.

The Three Ladies appear, wearing veils. The First Lady carries an urn with water, the second a stone, and the third a padlock and a medallion containing portrait.

DREI DAMEN:

Papageno!

PAPAGENO:
Aha, das geht mich an!
Sieh dich um, freund.

THE THREE LADIES:
(threatening and shouting in unison)
Papageno!

PAPAGENO:
Oh, they're calling me! *(to Tamino)*
Look around, friend.

TAMINO:
Wer sind diese Damen?

PAPAGENO:
Wer sie eigentlich sind, weiß ich selbst nicht. Ich weiß nur so viel, daß sie mir täglich meine Vögel abnehmen, und mir dafür Wein, Zuckerbrot und süße Feigen bringen.

TAMINO:
Sie sind vermutlich sehr schön?

PAPAGENO:
Ich denke nicht! Denn wann die schön wären, dann würden die noch nicht ihre Gesichter bedecken.

DREI DAMEN:
Papageno!

PAPAGENO:
Sei still! Sie drohen mir schon.

Ah, du fragst, ob sie schön sind, da kann ich dir nichts anderes darauf antworten, als daß ich in meinem Leben nichts reizenderes gesehen habe.
Jetzt werd ich gleich wieder gut sein.

DREI DAMEN:
Papageno!

PAPAGENO:
Was hab ich bloß heute verbrochen, daß die so aufgebracht wider mich sind?
Hier, meine Schönen, übergeb ich euch meine Vögel.

ERSTE DAME:

Dafür schickt dir unsere Fürstin heute zum ersten Mal statt Wein reines, helles Wasser.

TAMINO:
Who are these ladies?

PAPAGENO:
I really don't know who they are. I only know that everyday they take my birds from me, and in exchange, give me wine, cake, and sweet figs.

TAMINO:
Do you think they're very beautiful?

PAPAGENO:
I do not think so, because if they were beautiful they wouldn't cover their faces.

THE THREE LADIES: *(threatening)*
Papageno!

PAPAGENO: *(aside to Tamino)*
Be quiet! They're threatening me already.
(aloud)
Oh, you asked if they're beautiful. I can only tell you that in my whole life, I've never seen such beauties.
(to himself)
Now I'll behave myself again.

THREE LADIES:
Papageno!

PAPAGENO:
What in the world did I do wrong today to provoke them?
Here, lovely ladies, here are my birds.

FIRST LADY:
(Gives Papageno the urn with water)
In return, today our princess sends you clear water instead of wine.

ZWEITE DAME:
Und mir befahl sie, daß ich, statt Zuckerbrot, diesen Stein dir überbringen soll. Ich wünsche, daß er dir wohl bekommen möge.

PAPAGENO:
Was? Steine soll ich fressen?

DRITTE DAME:
Und statt der süßen Feigen, hab' ich die Ehre, dir dies goldene Schloß vor den Mund zu schlagen.

ERSTE DAME:
Du willst vermutlich wissen, warum die Fürstin dich heute so wunderbar bestraft?

ZWEITE DAME:
Damit du künftig nie mehr Fremde belügst.

DRITTE DAME:
Und daß du nie dich der Heldentaten rühmst, die andre vollzogen haben.

ERSTE DAME:
Sag an! Hast du diese Schlange bekämpft?

ZWEITE DAME:
Wer denn also?

THIRD LADY:
Wir waren's, Jüngling, die dich befreiten. Hier, dies Gemälde schickt dir die große Fürstin; es ist das Bildnis ihrer Tochter. "Findest du," sagte sie, "daß diese Züge dir nicht gleichgültig sind, dann ist Glück, Ehr' und Ruhm dein Los! Auf Wiedersehen.

SECOND LADY:
And I was ordered to give you this stone instead of cake. I hope you'll enjoy it.

PAPAGENO:
What? I have to eat stones now?

THIRD LADY:
And I have the honor, instead of sweet figs, to secure this golden padlock on your mouth.

FIRST LADY:
You undoubtedly want to know why the Queen is punishing you so wonderfully today?

(Papageno agrees by nodding his head)

SECOND LADY:
So that in the future you don't tell any more lies to strangers.

THIRD LADY:
And that you'll never again take credit for heroic deeds performed by others.

FIRST LADY:
Tell me! Did you fight this serpent?

(Papageno shakes no with his head)

SECOND LADY:
Well who did it then?

(Papageno indicates that he doesn't know)

THIRD LADY: *(to Tamino)*
Young man, we were the ones who rescued you. Here, the great Queen sends you this picture. It is a portrait of her daughter. She said that if you like what you see, happiness, honor, and fame will be yours! Farewell!

ZWEITE DAME:
Adieu, Monsieur Papageno!

SECOND LADY:
Goodbye, Mr. Papageno!
(The Second and Third Ladies take the birdcage and leave)

ERSTE DAME:
Fein nicht zu hastig getrunken!

FIRST LADY:
He didn't drink that so quickly!
(The First Lady leaves laughing)

Papageno hastens away in dumb astonishment.
Tamino becomes captivated by the portrait, and his love becomes intensified.

Dies Bild - nis ist bezanbernd schön, wie noch kein Au-ge je ge - sehn!

TAMINO:
Dies Bildnis ist bezanbernd schön,
wie noch kein Auge je gesehn!
Ich fühl es, wie dies Götterbild
mein Herz mit neuer Regung füllt.

Dies Etwas kann ich zwar nicht nennen,
doch fühl' ich's hier wie Feuer brennen.
Soll die Empfindung Liebe sein?
Ja, ja die Liebe ist's allein.

O wenn ich sie nur finden könnte!
O wenn sie doch schon vor mir stände!
Ich würde, würde, warm und rein.
Was würde ich?
Ich würde sie voll Entzücken
an diesen heißen Busen drücken,
und ewig wäre sie dann mein!

TAMINO:
No one has ever seen such magical beauty
as in this portrait!
As I look at this divine picture, my heart
beats excitedly.

I don't know what to call this feeling,
but its like a fire burning inside of me.
Is this what love feels like?
Yes, yes, this can only be love.

Oh, if I could only find her!
Oh, if she were already here!
Then I would be faithful and true.
What would I do?
I would charm her, and hold her against my
warm heart, and she would be mine
forever!

As it grows dark, there is a short, loud clap of thunder.
Tamino wants to leave, but the Three Ladies reappear.

Ihr Götter! Was ist das?

Good God! What is that?

ERSTE DAME:
Rüste dich mit Mut und Standhaftigkeit,
schöner Jüngling!
Die Fürstin....

ZWEITE DAME:
... hat mir aufgetragen, dir zu sagen...

DRITTE DAME:
daß der Weg zu deinem künftigen Glücke
nunmehr gebahnt sei.

ERSTE DAME:
Sie hat jedes deiner Worte gehört; Sie hat...

ZWEITE DAME:
...jeden Zug in deinem Gesichte gelesen...

DRITTE DAME:
...hat beschlossen, dich ganz glücklich zu
machen.

ERSTE DAME:
"Hat dieser Jüngling," sprach sie, "auch so
viel Mut und Tapferkeit, als er zärtlich ist, O,
so ist meine Tochter ganz gewiß gerettet."

TAMINO:
Gerettet?

ERSTE DAME:
Ein mächtiger, böser Dämon hat sie ihr
entrissen.

TAMINO:
Entrissen?
Sagt, sagt, wo ist des Tyrannen aufenthalt?

ZWEITE DAME:
Sehr nahe an unsern Bergen. Seine Burg ist
sorgsam bewacht.

TAMINO:
Pamina sei gerettet! Das schwör' ich bei
meiner Liebe, bei meinem Herzen.

FIRST LADY:
Prepare yourself with courage and
steadfastness, handsome young man!
The Queen...

SECOND LADY:
...has ordered me to tell you...

THIRD LADY:
that from now on, the road to your
future happiness is paved.

FIRST LADY:
She has heard every word you said, and she
has....

SECOND LADY:
...read every feature in your face...

THIRD LADY:
...and has decided to make you very happy.

FIRST LADY:
The Queen said: "if this young man has as
much courage and bravery as he is tender, oh,
then my daughter will definitely be rescued."

TAMINO:
Rescued?

FIRST LADY:
She was kidnapped by a strong and angry
demon.

TAMINO:
Kidnapped?
Tell me, where does this tyrant live?

THIRD LADY:
Very near our mountains. His fortress is
cautiously guarded.

TAMINO:
Pamina will be rescued! I swear it by my
heart and by my love.

Ihr Götter, was ist das?

DIE DREI DAMEN:
Fasse dich!

ERSTE DAME:
Es verkündigt die Ankunft unserer Königin.

DREI DAMEN:
Sie kommt! Sie kommt! Sie kommt!

(Short thunderclaps are heard)
Oh God, what is that?

THE THREE LADIES:
Be calm!

FIRST LADY:
It announces the arrival of our Queen.

(Thunder roars)
THREE LADIES:
She's coming! She's coming! She's coming!

Amidst the stars in the sky, the Queen of the Night appears.

KÖNIGIN DER NACHT:
O zittre nicht, mein lieber Sohn!
Du bist unschuldig, weise, fromm;
Ein Jüngling so wie du vermag am besten,
Dies tiefbetrübte Mutterherz zu trösten.

QUEEN OF THE NIGHT:
Oh don't be frightened, beloved son!
You are innocent, devout and wise.
A young man like you surely knows how to
comfort this deeply saddened mother's heart.

Larghetto
QUEEN OF THE NIGHT

Zum Lei - den bin ich auserkoren, denn meine Tochter fehlet mir.

Zum Leiden bin ich auserkoren,
denn meine Tochter fehlet mir;
durch sie ging all mein Glück verloren,
ein Bösewicht entfloh mit ihr.
Noch seh ich ihr Zittern Mit bangem
Erschüttern, ihr ängstliches Beben,
ihr schüchternes Streben. Ich mußte sie mir rauben sehen,
Ach helft! ach helft! war alles, was sie sprach. Allein vergebens war ihr Flehen,
Denn meine Hilfe war zu schwach.

Du, du, du wirst sie zu befreien gehen,
Du wirst der Tochter Retter sein.
Und werd' ich dich als Sieger sehen,
So sei sie dann auf ewig dein.

I have been doomed to suffer, and all of my happiness has disappeared since my daughter was kidnapped.
As a scoundrel abducted her, I still see her shiver, tremble, and quiver, with no strength to resist.

As I watched her being kidnapped, all she said was oh help me, oh help me. Her pleading was all in vain, since I was too weak to help her.

You, you, you will go and rescue her.
You will be the rescuer of my daughter.
And if you succeed, she will be yours forever.

As thunder roars, the Queen and the Three Ladies disappear.

TAMINO:
Ist's denn auch Wirklichkeit, was ich sah?
O ihr guten Götter, täuscht mich nicht!

PAPAGENO:

Hm, hm, hm, hm, hm!

TAMINO:
Der Arme kann von Strafe sagen, denn
seine Sprache ist dahin.

PAPAGENO:
Hm, hm, hm, hm, hm, hm!

TAMINO:
Ich kann nichts tun, als dich beklagen,
weil ich zu schwach zu helfen bin.

PAPAGENO:
Hm! Hm! Hm! Hm! Hm! Hm! Hm!

TAMINO:
Was that real?
Oh dear God, don't deceive me!

PAPAGENO:
(pointing sadly at the padlock on his mouth)
Hm, hm, hm, hm, hm, hm!

TAMINO:
The poor man was guilty of lying, and as a
penalty he can't talk anymore.

PAPAGENO:
Hm! hm! hm! hm! hm! hm! hm!

TAMINO:
I can't do anything but sympathize with
you, because I'm powerless to help you.

PAPAGENO:
Hm! Hhm! Hm! Hm! Hm! Hm! Hm!

The Three Ladies reappear. The First Lady carries a flute and chimes.

ERSTE DAME:
Die Königin begnadigt dich,
erläßt die Strafe dir durch mich.

PAPAGENO:
Nun plaudert Papageno wieder!

ZWEITE DAME:
Ja, plaudert! Lüge nur nicht wieder!

PAPAGENO:
Ich lüge nimmer mehr, nein, nein!

DREI DAMEN:
Dies Schloß soll deine Warnung sein.

PAPAGENO:
Dies Schloß soll meine Warnung sein.

THE FIRST LADY: *(to Papageno)*
I bring you the Queen's forgivenes and
pardon..

(She takes the padlock from his mouth)

PAPAGENO:
Now Papageno can chatter again!

SECOND LADY:
Yes, chatter! But never lie again!

PAPAGENO:
I'll never lie again, not ever!

THREE LADIES:
Let this padlock be your warning!

PAPAGENO:
This padlock shall be my warning.

ALLE:

Bekämen doch die Lügner alle
ein solches Schloß vor ihren Mund;
statt Haß, Verleumdung, schwarzer Galle,
bestünden Lieb' und Bruderbund.

ERSTE DAME

O Prinz, nimm dies Geschenk von mir!
Dies sendet uns're Fürstin dir.
Die Zauberflöte wird dich schützen,
im größten Unglück unterstützen.

DREI DAMEN:

Hiermit kannst du allmächtig handeln,
der Menschen Leidenschaft verwandeln:
der Traurige wird freudig sein,
den Hagestolz nimmt Liebe ein.

ALLE:

O so eine Flöte ist mehr als Gold und Kronen
wert, denn durch sie wird Menschenglück und
Zufriedenheit vermehrt.

PAPAGENO:

Nun, ihr schönen Frauenzimmer,
darf ich, so empfehl' ich mich.

DREI DAMEN:

Dich empfehlen kannst du immer, doch
bestimmt die Fürstin dich, mit dem Prinzen
ohn' Velweilen nach Sarastros Burg zu
eilen.

PAPAGENO:

Nein, dafür bedank' ich mich!
Von euch selbsten hörte ich, daß er wie ein
Tigertier. Sicher ließ' ohn' alle Gnaden
Mich Sarastro rupfen, braten, Setzte mich
den Hunden für.

DREI DAMEN:

Dich schützt der Prinz, trau' ihm allein.
Dafür sollst du sein Diener sein.

ALL:

If only all liars would get such a lock on
their mouths, then we would have love and
friendship instead of hate and slander.

FIRST LADY:

(gives Tamino a golden flute)
Oh Prince, take this gift from me! Our
Queen commanded us to give it to you. This
Magic Flute will protect you in danger and
support you in your deepest sorrow.

THE THREE LADIES:

With this flute you will possess divine powers.
You can reverse human suffering, convert
sadness to happiness, and assure that the
loveless will always be loved.

ALL:

Oh, such a flute is worth its weight in gold,
because it brings untold happiness and
contentment to humanity.

PAPAGENO:

And now beautiful ladies, if I may, I'd like
to leave.

THE THREE LADIES:

You can always leave, but the Queen
commands you and the Prince to hurry to
Sarastro's castle without delay.

PAPAGENO:

No thank you!
I myself heard you say that he's like a tiger.
Surely Sarastro would have me
unmercifully plucked and roasted, and I'd
become a tasty meal for his dogs.

THE THREE LADIES:

Trust the Prince, for he'll protect you, You'll
be his faithful servant.

PAPAGENO:
Daß doch der Prinz beim Teufel wäre!
Mein Leben ist mir lieb;
Am Ende schleicht, bei meiner Ehre,
Er von mir wie ein Dieb.

ERSTE DAME:

Hier, nimm dies Kleinod, es ist dein.

PAPAGENO:
Ei, ei! Was mag darinnen sein?

DREI DAMEN:
Darinnen hörst du Glöckchen tönen.

PAPAGENO:
Werd' ich sie auch wohl spielen können?

DREI DAMEN:
O ganz gewiß! Ja, ja, gewiß!

ALLE FÜNF:
Silberglöckchen, Zauberflöten
Sind zu eurem/unserm Schutz vonnöten.
Lebet wohl! Wir wollen gehn.
Lebet wohl, auf Wiedersehn!

TAMINO:
Doch, schöne Damen, saget an...

PAPAGENO:
Wie man die Burg wohl finden kann?

BEIDE:
Wie man die Burg wohl finden kann?

DREI DAMEN:
Drei Knäbchen, jung, schön, hold und
weise, Umschweben euch auf eurer Reise.
Sie werden eure Führer sein,
Folgt ihrem Rate ganz allein.

TAMINO, PAPAGENO:
Drei Knäbchen, jung, schön, hold und weise,
Umschweben uns auf unserer Reise.

PAPAGENO: *(to himself)*
Maybe the Prince would risk his life, but I
don't want to lose mine. And finally, he
may well disappear on me when I need
him.

FIRST LADY: *(presents Papageno with a
box containing chimes: the glockenspiel)*
Here, take this treasure, it's yours.

PAPAGENO:
Oh, oh, what could be inside?

THE THREE LADIES:
You can hear the bells ringing inside.

PAPAGENO:
And would I be able to play them too?

THE THREE LADIES:
Oh very definitely! Yes, yes, definitely!

ALL FIVE:
Silver bells and magic flutes are your/our
protection.
Farewell! We're leaving.
Farewell, till we meet again!

TAMINO:
But beautiful Ladies, could you please tell us..

PAPAGENO:
...where this castle is?

BOTH:
How to find the way to this great castle?

THE THREE LADIES:
Three handsome, kind, and wise young
boys will surround you and show you the
way. Be sure to follow their advice!

TAMINO AND PAPAGENO:
Three handsome, kind, and wise young boys
will surround us and show us the way.

DREI DAMEN:
Sie werden eure Führer sein,
Folgt ihrem Rate ganz allein.

ALLE:
So lebet wohl! Wir wollen gehn.
Lebt wohl, lebt wohl, auf Wiederseh'n!

THREE LADIES:
They will be your guide. Make sure to
follow their advice.

ALL:
Farewell! We're leaving.
Farewell, farewell, till we meet again!

All depart

ACT I - Scene 2

A room in Sarastro's palace.

SKLAVE:
Ha, ha, ha! Unser Peiniger, der alles
belauschende Mohr, wird morgen sicherlich
gehangen oder gespießt! Pamina entfloh vor
seinen Augen. So ist der Mohr nichts mehr
zu retten, auch wenn Pamina von Sarastros
Gefolge wieder eingefangen würde.

SLAVES:
Ha, ha, ha! Our tyrant, the Moor, will
surely be hung or speared in the morning,
because Pamina escaped from right under
his eyes. Nothing can save the Moor now,
even if Sarastro's men would recapture her.

MONOSTATOS:
He, Sklaven! Schafft Fesseln herbei!

MONOSTATOS:
Hey, Slaves, bring the handcuffs!

SKLAVE:
Fesseln? Doch nicht für Pamina? Der
unbarmherzige Teufel, wie der sie bei den
Händen faßt. Das halt ich nicht aus.

SLAVES:
Handcuffs? We hope they're not for
Pamina? I can't stand it, how the heartless
devil mistreats her.

MONOSTATOS:
Du feines Täubchen, nur herein!

(Pamina is brought in by the Slaves)
MONOSTATOS:
Come in you lovely little dove!

PAMINA:
O welche Marter, welche Pein!

PAMINA:
What torture and pain!

MONOSTATOS:
Verloren ist dein Leben!

MONASTATOS:
Your life is over!

PAMINA:
Der Tod macht mich nicht beben, nur
meine Mutter dauert mich; sie stirbt vor
Gram ganz sicherlich.

MONOSTATOS:
He, Sklaven, legt ihr Fesseln an!
Mein Haß soll dich verderben!

PAMINA:
O laßt mich lieber sterben, Weil nichts,
Barbar, dich rühren kann!

MONOSTATOS:
Nun fort! Laßt mich bei ihr allein!

PAPAGENO:
Wo bin ich wohl? Wo mag ich sein?
Aha! da find' ich Leute, gewagt, ich geh'
hinein.

PAMINA:
I'm not afraid to die. I only feel sorry for
my mother, since she will certainly die
from grief.

MONASTATOS:
Hey, Slaves, shackle her!
My hatred will destroy you!

PAMINA:
Tyrant, since you have no compassion, I
prefer to die.

(Pamina becomes unconscious)
MONASTATOS: *(to the Slaves)*
Go away! Leave me alone with her!

PAPAGENO: *(from outside)*
Where am I? Where can I be?
Aha! I see some people, I guess I'll venture
in.

Papageno enters the room and notices Pamina.

Schön Mädchen, jung und rein,
viel weißer noch als Kreide.

Oh what a beauty, so young and pure, and
whiter than snow.

*Monostatos turns around. Papageno is terrified by Monostatos's gaze,
and each becomes frightened by the other.*

MONOSTATOS UND PAPAGENO:
Hu! Das ist der Teufel sicherlich!
Hab' Mitleid! Verschone mich!
Hu, hu, hu!

MONOSTATOS and PAPAGENO:
Ay! That's the devil for sure!
Have pity! Spare me!
Ay! Ay! Ay!

They both run away, looking back at each other cautiously over their shoulders.

PAMINA:
Mutter - Mutter - Mutter!

PAMINA: *(dreamlike)*
Mother! Mother! Mother!
(She regains consciousness)

Wie? Noch schlägt dieses Herz? Zu neuen
Qualen erwacht?
O das ist hart, sehr hart! Mir bitterer, als der
Tod.

What? This heart is still beating? Did it
awaken to new tortures?
Oh, it's so cruel, so cruel! It's worse than
death!

PAPAGENO
Bin ich nicht ein Narr, daß ich mich
schrecken ließ?
Es gibt doch auch schwarze Vögel auf der Welt,
warum denn nicht auch schwarze Menschen?

Ah, da ist ja das schöne Fräuleinbild noch.
Du Tochter der nächtlichen Königin!

PAMINA:
Nächtlichen Königin? Wer bist du?

PAPAGENO:
Ein Abgesandter der sternflammenden
Königin.

PAMINA:
Meiner Mutter? O Wonne!
Dein Name?

PAPAGENO:
Papageno.

PAMINA:
Papageno? Papageno. Ich erinnere mich,
den Namen oft gehört zu haben, dich selbst
aber sah ich nie.

PAPAGENO:
Ich dich ebensowenig.

PAMINA:
Du kennst also meine gute, zärtliche Mutter?

PAPAGENO:
Wenn du die Tochter der nächtlichen
Königin bist, ja!

PAMINA:
O ich bin es.

PAPAGENO:
Das will ich gleich erkennen.

(Papageno carefully enters)
PAPAGENO:
Am I not a fool to let myself be frightened?
There are black birds in this world, so why
not black people?

(He notices Pamina)
Ah, here's the lovely maiden in the portrait!
The daughter of the Queen of Night!

PAMINA:
Queen of the Night? Who are you?

PAPAGENO:
A messenger from the star-flaming Queen.

PAMINA:
From my mother? How wonderful!
What is your name?

PAPAGENO:
Papageno.

PAMINA:
Papageno? Papageno. I remember having
heard that name often, but I never met you
personally.

PAPAGENO:
I've never met you either.

PAMINA:
So you know my good and loving mother?

PAPAGENO:
If you are the daughter of the Queen of the
Night, yes!

PAMINA:
Yes it's me.

PAPAGENO:
Let me see if it's true.

Papageno examines the portrait that Tamino received from the Three Ladies, which he wears on a ribbon around his neck.

Die Augen schwarz - richtig, schwarz.
Die Lippen rot - richtig rot.
Blonde Haare - blonde Haare.
Alles trifft ein, bis auf Hände und Füße.
Nach dem Gemälde zu schließen,
sollst du weder Hände noch Füße haben;
denn hier sind keine angezegt.

Blue eyes - very blue.
Red lips-very red.
Blond hair-blond hair.
Everything matches, except the hands and feet. According to the portrait you wouldn't have hands or feet because they don't show here.

PAMINA:
Erlaube mir. Ja, ich bin's! Wie kam es in deine Hände?

PAMINA:
Permit me. Yes, it's me! But how did you get it?

PAPAGENO:
Ich muß dir das umständlicher erzählen. Ich kam heute früh, wie gewöhnlich, zu deiner Mutter Palast mit meiner Lieferung.

PAPAGENO:
I must tell you the details of what happened. As usual, I went this morning to your mother's palace to make my delivery.

PAMINA:
Lieferung?

PAMINA:
Delivery?

PAPAGENO:
Ja, ich liefere deiner Mutter schon seit vielen Jahren alle die schönen Vögel in den Palast.

Ja, und eben, als ich im Begriffe war, meine Vögel abzugeben, da seh ich einen Menschen vor mir, der sich Prinz nennen läßt, und dieser Prinz hat deine Mutter so von sich eingenommen, daß sie ihm dein Bildnis schenkte und ihm befahl, dich zu befreien.

Sein Entschluß, der war ebenso rasch, als seine Liebe zu dir.

PAPAGENO:
Yes, for years I've been delivering all the beautiful birds to your mother at the palace.

You know, just as I was delivering the birds, I saw someone who identified himself as a Prince. The Prince so impressed your mother, that she gave him your portrait and ordered him to rescue you.

He fell in love with you, and immediately resolved to rescue you.

PAMINA:
Liebe?
Er liebt mich also? O sage mir das noch einmal, ich höre das Wort Liebe gar zu gerne.

PAMINA:
Love?
Then he loves me? Please repeat that to me again, because I love to hear the sound of that word.

PAPAGENO:
Das glaube ich dir. Bist ja auch ein Fräuleinbild. Kurz also, diese große Liebe zu dir war der Peitschenstreich, um unsre Füße im schnellen Gang zu bringen, und nun sind wir hier, dir tausend schöne und angenehme Sachen zu sagen.

PAMINA:
Freund, wenn Sarastro dich hier erblicken sollte, dann....

PAPAGENO:
So würde mir meine Rückreise erspart blieben - das kann ich mir denken.

PAMINA:
Dein martervoller Tod würde ohne Grenzen sein.

PAPAGENO:
Um diesem auszuweichen, gehn wir lieber beizeiten.

PAMINA:
Wir haben keine Minute zu versäumen.

PAPAGENO:
Ja, komm, du wirst Augen machen, wenn du den schönen Jüngling erblickst.

PAMINA:
Aber wenn dies ein Fallstrick wäre - wenn dieser nun ein böser Geist von Sarastros Gefolge wäre?

PAPAGENO:
Was? Ich ein böser Geist? Wo denkst du hin? Ich bin der beste Geist von der Welt.

PAMINA:
Vergib, vergib, wenn ich dich beleidigte! Du hast ein gefühlvolles Herz.

PAPAGENO:
I believe you because you're a young girl, and therefore the idea of love strikes you like a thunderbolt that urges you to seduce men to cater to you, and shower you with sweet words.

PAMINA:
If Sarastro would see you here, my friend, then....

PAPAGENO:
Then, I have the feeling that I'll never return home.

PAMINA:
You would suffer an agonizing death.

PAPAGENO:
To save our lives, we'd better leave right away.

PAMINA:
We can't waste a minute.

PAPAGENO:
Let's go, you won't believe your eyes when you see this handsome young man.

PAMINA:
But what if this is a trick, and you're a villain employed by Sarastro?

PAPAGENO:
What? Me, a villain? What are you thinking? I'm the most honorable man on earth.

PAMINA:
I'm sorry, forgive me if I have offended you! You're a very sensitive person.

PAPAGENO:
Ja, freilich habe ich ein gefühlvolles Herz! Aber was nutzt mir denn das alles? - Ich möcht' mir doch oft alle meine Federn ausrupfen, wenn ich bedenk', daß Papageno noch keine Papagena hat.

PAMINA:
Armer Mann! Du hast also noch kein Weib?

PAPAGENO:
Noch nicht einmal ein Mädchen, geschweige denn ein Weib! Und unsereiner hat eben auch so seine lustigen Stunden, wo man so richtig so gesellschaftliche Unterhaltung haben möcht'.

PAMINA:
Geduld, Freund! Der Himmel wird auch für dich sorgen; er wird dir eine Freundin schicken, ehe du dir's vermutest.

PAPAGENO:
Wenn er's nur bald schickte!

PAPAGENO:
Yes, I am very sensitive, but what good is it? I sometimes want to pluck out all my feathers when I think about the fact that there still is no Mrs. Papageno.

PAMINA:
Poor man! So you don't have a wife yet?

PAPAGENO:
Not even a girlfriend, let alone a wife. And every one of us has happy moments which he would like to share with someone he loves.

PAMINA:
Patience, my friend! Heaven will take care of you too, and send you a girlfriend before you know it.

PAPAGENO:
If only it would happen soon!

Andantino
PAMINA
Bei Männern, welche Lie - be fühlen, fehlt auch ein gu - tes Her - ze nicht.

PAMINA:
Bei Männern, welche Liebe fühlen, fehlt auch ein gutes Herze nicht.

PAPAGENO:
Die süßen Triebe mitzufühlen, ist dann der Weiber erste Pflicht.

BEIDE:
Wir wollen uns der Liebe freun, wir leben durch die Lieb' allein.

PAMINA:
Die Lieb' versüßet jede Plage, ihr opfert jede Kreatur.

PAMINA:
Men who experience love also possess a good heart.

PAPAGENO:
And it's a wife's priority to share those sensibilities.

BOTH:
It's love alone that makes us happy, and it's love alone that makes life worthwhile.

PAMINA:
Whatever will happen, it is love that will heal every sorrow.

PAPAGENO:
Sie würzet unsre Lebenstage, sie wirkt im
Kreise der Natur.

BEIDE:
Ihr hoher Zweck zeigt deutlich an,
nichts Edler's sei, als Weib und Mann.
Mann und Weib, und Weib und Mann
reichen an die Gottheit an.

PAPAGENO:
Love perfumes life with its rare fragrance, and it's human nature to love.

BOTH:
For husband and wife, the highest goal in
life is the nobility of love. For husband
and wife, and for wife and husband,
love becomes a divine union.

Pamina and Papageno exit.

ACT I - Scene 3

*A sacred grove in which there are three temples:
the Temple of Wisdom, the Temple of Reason, and the Temple of Nature.*

*The Three Youths appear bearing silver palm branches.
They accompany Tamino whose flute hangs at his side.*

DREI KNABEN:
Zum Ziele führt dich diese Bahn, doch
mußt du, Jüngling, männlich siegen. Drum
höre unsre Lehre an: Sei standhaft,
duldsam und verschwiegen!

THE THREE YOUTHS:
This path will lead you to your goal, young
man, but you must be courageous!.
Listen to our advice and be firm, patient,
and discreet.

TAMINO:
Ihr holden Kleinen, sagt mir an, ob ich
Pamina retten kann?

TAMINO:
Tell me boys, do you think that I can rescue
Pamina?

DREI KNABEN:
Dies kundzutun, steht uns nicht an:
Sei standhaft, duldsam und verschwiegen!
Bedenke dies; kurz, sei ein Mann,
Dann, Jüngling, wirst du männlich siegen.

THE THREE YOUTHS:
We don't know, but just be steadfast,
patient and discreet! In short, think of this:
be a man, and you, young man, will
succeed like a man.

The Three Youths depart, leaving Tamino alone.

TAMINO:
Die Weisheitslehre dieser Knaben
Sei ewig mir ins Herz gegraben.
Wo bin ich nun? Was wird mit mir?
Ist dies der Sitz der Götter hier?
Doch zeigen die Pforten, es zeigen die
Säulen, Daß Klugheit und Arbeit und
Künste hier weilen. Wo Tätigkeit thronet
und Müßiggang weicht, erhält seine
Herrschaft das Laster nicht leicht.

Ich wage mich mutig zur Pforte hinein,
die Absicht ist edel und lauter und rein.
Erzitt're, feiger Bösewicht!
Pamina retten ist mir Pflicht.

TAMINO:
I will never forget the wisdom that these
boys taught me.
Where am I now? What will happen to
me? Is this perhaps where the gods
reside?
The portals and columns show that
intelligence and art exist here, and that it
is a place where industry dominates and
vice is nonexistent.

I'll boldly enter through the temple door.
My purpose is noble, good, and pure.
Tremble wretched villain!
To rescue Pamina's is my duty.

He approaches the temple at the right

STIMME:
Zurück!

A VOICE:
Go back!

TAMINO:
Zurück? Zurück? So wag' ich hier mein
Glück!

TAMINO:
Go back? Go back? Then I'll try my luck
over there!

He goes to the temple at the left.

STIMME:
Zurück!

VOICE:
Go back!

TAMINO:
Auch hier ruft man: Zurück!

TAMINO:
Here too they call go back!

He goes to the middle Temple of Wisdom.

Da seh' ich noch eine Tür, Vielleicht find'
ich den Eingang hier.

I see another door over there. Maybe I'll be
able to enter there.

The middle door opens and an old Priest emerges.

ÄLTERER PRIESTER:
Wo willst du, kühner Fremdling, hin?
Was suchst du hier im Heiligtum?

ELDERLY PRIEST:
Where do you want to go, daring stranger?
What are you looking for in this sanctuary?

TAMINO:
Der Lieb' und Tugend Eigentum.

ÄLTERER PRIESTER:
Die Worte sind von hohem Sinn!
Allein wie willst du diese finden?
Dich leitet Lieb' und Tugend nicht,
Weil Tod und Rache dich entzünden.

TAMINO:
Nur Rache für den Bösewicht.

ÄLTERER PRIESTER:
Den wirst du wohl bei uns nicht finden.

TAMINO:
Sarastro herrscht in diesen Gründen?

ÄLTERER PRIESTER:
Ja, ja! Sarastro herrschet hier.

TAMINO:
Doch in dem Weisheitstempel nicht?

ÄLTERER PRIESTER:
Er herrscht im Weisheitstempel hier!

TAMINO:
So ist denn alles Heuchelei!

ÄLTERER PRIESTER:
Willst du schon wieder gehn?

TAMINO:
Ja, ich will gehen, froh und frei, nie euren Tempel seh'n!

ÄLTERER PRIESTER:
Erklär dich näher mir, dich täuschet ein Betrug.

TAMINO:
Sarastro wohnt hier, das ist mir schon genug!

TAMINO:
A place of virtue and of love.

ELDERLY PRIEST:
Your words are certainly noble!
But how do you expect to find these?
You're not guided by love and courage,
but by death and vengeance.

TAMINO:
I'm guided by vengeance on the villain.

ELDERLY PRIEST:
You surely will not find him here.

TAMINO:
Doesn't Sarastro rule here?

ELDERLY PRIEST:
Yes, yes! Sarastro rules here.

TAMINO:
In the Temple of Wisdom?

ELDERLY PRIEST:
Yes, in the Temple of Wisdom!

TAMINO:
So then all of this is hypocrisy!
(Tamino wants to leave)

ELDERLY PRIEST:
You want to leave already?

TAMINO:
Yes, I want to leave, happy and free, and I never want to see your temple again.

ELDERLY PRIEST:
Explain yourself to me! You are deluded by deceit.

TAMINO:
The fact that Sarastro lives here is enough for me.

ÄLTERER PRIESTER:
Wenn du dein Leben liebst, so rede, bleibe da! Sarastro hassest du?

TAMINO:
Ich haß ihn ewig, ja!

ÄLTERER PRIESTER:
Nun gib mir deine Gründe an.

TAMINO:
Er ist ein Unmensch, ein Tyrann!

ÄLTERER PRIESTER:
Ist das, was du gesagt, erwiesen?

TAMINO:
Durch ein unglücklich Weib bewiesen,
Das Gram und Jammer niederdrückt.

ÄLTERER PRIESTER:
Ein Weib hat also dich berückt?
Ein Weib tut wenig, plaudert viel.
Du, Jüngling, glaubst dem Zungenspiel?

O legte doch Sarastro dir die Absicht seiner Handlung für!

TAMINO:
Die Absicht ist nur allzu klar!
Riß nicht der Räuber ohn' Erbarmen,
mina aus der Mutter Armen?

ÄLTERER PRIESTER:
Ja, Jüngling, was du sagst, ist wahr.

TAMINO:
Wo ist sie, die er uns geraubt?
Man opferte vielleicht sie schon?

ÄLTERER PRIESTER:
Dir dies zu sagen, teurer Sohn, ist jetztund mir noch nicht erlaubt.

TAMINO:
Erklär dies Rätsel, täusch' mich nicht!

ELDERLY PRIEST:
If you value your life, speak and stay here! Do you hate Sarastro?

TAMINO:
I hate him intensely, and I always will!

ELDERLY PRIEST:
Give me your reasons for that!

TAMINO:
He is a brute and a tyrant!

ELDERLY PRIEST:
Do you have proof of what you just said?

TAMINO:
It was proven to me by an unhappy woman, oppressed by great sorrow.

ELDERLY PRIEST:
So a woman tricked you?
Women do little and talk too much.
You believe this nonsense?

Sarastro has clearly explained the motives for his action.

TAMINO:
His motive is all too clear!
Didn't the kidnapper tear Pamina unmercifully from her mother's arms?

ELDERLY PRIEST:
Yes, young man, what you say is true.

TAMINO:
Where is the kidnapped victim?
Has she been sacrificed already?

ELDERLY PRIEST:
That my dear boy, I am not allowed to tell you yet.

TAMINO:
Explain this riddle! Don't deceive me!

ÄLTERER PRIESTER:
Die Zunge bindet Eid und Pflicht.

ELDERLY PRIEST:
Oath and duty forbid me to talk.

TAMINO:
Wann also wird die Decke schwinden?

TAMINO:
When will you be able to talk?

ÄLTERER PRIESTER:
Sobald dich führt der Freundschaft Hand
In's Heiligtum zum ew'gen Band.

ELDERLY PRIEST:
As soon as the hand of friendship leads you
into the sanctuary of the sacred brotherhood.

The Elderly Priest departs.

TAMINO
O ew'ge Nacht! Wann wirst du
schwinden? Wann wird das Licht mein
Auge finden?

TAMINO: *(alone.)*
Oh, eternal night! When will you disappear? When will daylight come?

STIMMEN:
Bald, Jüngling, oder nie!

VOICES: *(from inside the middle temple)*
Soon, young man, or never!

TAMINO:
Bald, sagt ihr, oder nie? Ihr Unsichtbaren,
saget mir, lebt denn Pamina noch?

TAMINO:
Soon, you say, or never? Tell me, invisible
ones, is Pamina still alive?

STIMMEN:
Pamina lebet noch!

VOICES:
Pamina is still alive!

TAMINO:
Sie lebt! Ich danke euch dafür.

TAMINO: *(happily)*
She's alive! Thank you so much.

O wenn ich doch imstande wäre,
allmächtige, zu eurer Ehre, mit jedem Tone
meinen Dank zu schildern, wie er hier, entsprang.

(Tamino takes his flute in his hand.)
Oh, almighty ones, if only I had the
opportunity to honor you and express my
thanks with each tone of my flute.

*Tamino plays the flute, and wild animals and birds of every kind appear to listen.
When he stops playing, they flee.*

Wie stark ist nicht dein Zauberton,
weil, holde Flöte, durch dein Spielen
selbst wilde Tiere Freude fühlen.
Doch Pamina, nur Pamina bleibt davon!

The sweet melodious tones of your magic
flute have the power to even delight wild
animals.
But only Pamina doesn't come!
(Tamino plays the flute again)

Pamina! Pamina! Höre, höre mich! Umsonst!	Pamina! Pamina! Listen to me playing! It's hopeless!
	(Replays)
Wo? Ach, wo find' ich dich?	Where? Oh, where can I find you?
	(Papageno's flute is heard)
Ha, das ist Papagenos Ton!	Aha, that's the sound of Papageno's flute!

Tamino replays his flute, and Papageno answers as before.

Vielleicht sah er Pamina schon,	Maybe he's seen Pamina already.
Vielleicht eilt sie mit ihm zu mir!	Maybe she's coming with him.
Vielleicht führt mich der Ton zu ihr.	Maybe these flute tones will lead me to her.

Tamino leaves. Papageno and Pamina appear. Monostatos pursues them.

PAMINA, PAPAGENO:
Schnelle Füße, rascher Mut
schützt vor Feindes List und Wut.
Fänden wir Tamino doch,
sonst erwischen sie uns noch.

PAMINA:
Holder Jüngling!

PAPAGENO:
Stille, stille, ich kann's besser!

PAMINA AND PAPAGENO:
Quick steps and dauntless courage may
save us from the foe's dreadful rage.
If only we could find Tamino, otherwise
we'll surely be captured!

PAMINA: *(calling to Tamino)*
Handsome young man!

PAPAGENO:
Quiet, I can do it better.

Papageno whistles, and Tamino answers with his flute.

BEIDE:
Welche Freude ist wohl größer?
Freund Tamino hört uns schon.

Hierher kam der Flötenton.
Welch ein Glück, wenn ich ihn finde.
Nur geschwinde! Nur geschwinde!

BOTH:
Could anything make me happier?
Our friend Tamino hears us now.
(pointing in the direction)
There's where the flute sounds came from.
Oh, how wonderful if I would find him!
Let's hurry! Let's hurry!

Monostatos confronts them.

MONOSTATOS:
Nur geschwinde! Nur geschwinde!
Ha, hab' ich euch noch erwischt?

Nur herbei mit Stahl und Eisen.

Wart', ich will euch Mores weisen.
den Monostatos berücken!
Nur herbei mit Band und Stricken,
he, ihr Sklaven, kommt herbei!

MONOSTATOS: *(mocking Pamina)*
Let's hurry! Let's hurry!
Ha, ha, I've caught you?
(calling his Slaves)
Quickly, chain them!
(to Pamina and Papageno)
Wait, I'll show you how to deceive
Monostatos!
Slaves, come over here and chain them!.

PAMINA, PAPAGENO:
Ach, nun ist's mit uns vorbei!

PAMINA, PAPAGENO:
Oh, we're finished!

PAPAGENO:
Wer viel wagt, gewinnt oft viel!
Komm, du schönes Glockenspiel,
laß die Glöckchen klingen, klingen,
daß die Ohren ihnen singen.

PAPAGENO:
One who dares often gains alot!
Come, magic set of bells, let your tones fill
the air and resound in every ear.

(Papageno plays the Glockenspiel)

MONOSTATOS, SKLAVEN:

Das klinget so herrlich,
das klinget so schön!
Larala la la larala la la larala!
Nie hab' ich so etwas gehört und geseh'n!
Larala la la larala la la larala!

MONOSTATOS AND THE SLAVES:
(Subdued by the sound, Monostatos and the Slaves sing and dance.)
It sounds so delightful,
Its sound is so beautiful!
Tralala, lalala, tralalalala!
Oh, I've never heard anything like it!
Tralalala, trala lalala!

(They leave while singing and dancing)

PAMINA, PAPAGENO:
Könnte jeder brave Mann solche
Glöckchen finden!

Seine Feinde würden dann ohne Mühe
schwinden, und er lebte ohne sie
in der besten Harmonie!

Nur der Freundschaft Harmonie mildert die
Beschwerden; ohne diese Sympathie
ist kein Glück auf Erden.

PAPAGENO AND PAMINA:
If only everyone could own such magic
bells!

Then all enemies would easily disappear,
and without them, everyone would live
in great harmony!

Only the harmony of friendship softens
every misfortune. And without this good
feeling, there can be no happiness on earth.

A fanfare of trumpets and drums are heard.

CHOR:
Es lebe Sarastro! Sarastro lebe!

VOICES:
Long live Sarastro! Sarastro lives!

PAPAGENO:
Was soll das bedeuten? Ich zittre, ich bebe!

PAPAGENO:
What's all this about? I'm trembling and shuddering!

PAMINA:
O Freund, nun ist's um uns getan, dies kündigt den Sarastro an!

PAMINA:
Oh my friend, we're finished! It announces that Sarastro is coming!

PAPAGENO:
O wär ich eine Maus, wie wollt' ich mich verstecken!
Wär ich so klein wie Schnecken, so kröch' ich in mein Haus!
Mein Kind, was werden wir nun sprechen?

PAPAGENO:
Oh, if only I were a mouse, then I could hide!
If I were as small as a snail, I'd crawl in my house.
My dear child, what are we going to say?

PAMINA:
Die Wahrheit! Die Wahrheit, sei sie auch Verbrechen.

PAMINA:
The truth! The truth, no matter what!

(Sarastro enters with his retinue)

CHOR:
Es lebe Sarastro! Sarastro soll leben!
Er ist es, dem wir uns mit Freuden ergeben!
Stets mög' er des Lebens als Weiser sich freun,
er ist unser Abgott, dem alle sich weihn.

CHORUS:
Long live Sarastro! Sarastro shall live!
We are all devoted to him!
As a wise man, may he enjoy life forever.
He is our idol whom we worship and love!

PAMINA:
Herr, ich bin zwar Verbrecherin,
ich wollte deiner Macht entfliehn,
Allein die Schuld ist nicht an mir,
der böse Mohr verlangte Liebe;
darum, o Herr, entfloh ich dir.
Er ist's!

PAMINA: *(kneels)*
Oh Lord, it's true that I am guilty, because I wished to flee from your power.
But it's not my fault.
I escaped because the wicked Moor desired my love.
He is the guilty one!

SARASTRO:
Steh auf, erheitre dich, o Liebe!
Denn ohne erst in dich zu dringen,
weiß ich von deinem Herzen mehr:
du liebest einen andern sehr.
Zur Liebe will ich dich nicht zwingen,
doch geb' ich dir die Freiheit nicht.

SARASTRO:
Get up, my love, and be happy!
I need not question you further, for I know what is in your heart:
you already love another very much.
Although I will never compel you to love,
I cannot give you your freedom.

PAMINA:
Mich rufet ja die Kindespflicht,
denn meine Mutter...

SARASTRO:
...steht in meiner Macht. Du würdest um
dein Glück gebracht, wenn ich dich ihren
Händen ließe.

PAMINA:
Mir klingt der Muttername süße; sie ist es...

SARASTRO:
...und ein stolzes Weib!
Ein Mann muß eure Herzen leiten,
denn ohne ihn pflegt jedes Weib
aus ihrem Wirkungskreis zu schreiten.

MONOSTATOS:
Nun stolzer Jüngling, nur hierher!
Hier ist Sarastro, unser Herr.

PAMINA:
Er ist's!

TAMINO:
Sie ist's!

PAMINA:
Ich glaub' es kaum!

TAMINO:
Sie ist's!

PAMINA:
Er ist's!

TAMINO:
Es ist kein Traum!

PAMINA:
Es schling' mein Arm sich um ihn her!

PAMINA:
A child's duty calls me, because my
mother....

SARASTRO:
...is in my power. Your happiness would be
ended if I would return you to her.

PAMINA:
The mention of the word mother sounds so
sweet to me. It is she who is . . . .

SARASTRO:
...a haughty woman!
Only a man should guide women's hearts,
because without man, every woman would
stray.

MONOSTATOS: *(to Tamino)*
Proud young man, come here!
This is Sarastro, our dear lord.

PAMINA: *(seeing Tamino for the first time)*
It's him!

TAMINO: *(seeing Pamina)*
It's her!

PAMINA:
I can hardly believe it!

TAMINO:
It's her!

PAMINA:
It's him!

TAMINO:
It's not a dream!

(They approach each other)
PAMINA:
I would embrace him!

TAMINO:
Es schling' mein Arm sich um sie her!

BEIDE:
Und wenn es auch mein Ende wär!

ALLE:
Was soll das heißen?

MONOSTATOS:
Welch eine Dreistigkeit!

He steps between Pamina and Tamino, and separates them.

Gleich auseinander! Das geht zu weit!

Dein Sklave liegt zu deinen Füßen,
laß den verwegnen Frevler büßen!

Bedenk, wie frech der Knabe ist:

durch dieses seltnen Vogels List
wollt er Pamina dir entführen,
allein ich wußt' ihn auszuspüren.
Du kennst mich! Meine Wachsamkeit.

SARASTRO:
Verdient, daß man ihr Lorbeer streut!
He, gebt dem Ehrenmann sogleich.-

MONOSTATOS:
Schon deine Gnade macht mich reich.

SARASTRO:
Nur siebenundsiebenzig Sohlenstreich!

MONOSTATOS:
Ach Herr, den Lohn verhofft' ich nicht!

SARASTRO:
Nicht Dank, es ist ja meine Pfticht!

TAMINO:
I would embrace her!

BOTH:
Even if it would kill me!

(Pamina and Tamino)
ALL:
What does that mean?

MONOSTATOS:
How audacious!

That's enough! This is going too far!

(Monostatos kneels before Sarastro.)
Your slave kneels before you.
Penalize this presumptuous youth!

Think how impudent this boy is.
(Pointing at Papageno.)
Using the tricks of this rare bird, he wanted
to rob you of Pamina.
But I could track him down. You know me
and my vigilance.

SARASTRO:
He deserves the laurel wreath!
Here, give him his reward.

MONOSTATOS:
Your favor alone enriches me.

SARASTRO:
You're to get a whipping of seventy-seven lashes!

MONOSTATOS:
Ah, sir, I don't merit such a reward!

SARASTRO:
Save your thanks, it's only my duty.

ALLE:
Es lebe Sarastro, der göttliche Weise!
Er lohnet und strafet in ähnlichem Kreise.

ALL:
Long live Sarastro, the divine sage!
He justly punishes and rewards

SARASTRO:
Führt diese beiden Fremdlinge in unsern
Prüfungstempel ein; Bedecket ihre Häupter
dann, sie müssen erst gereinigt sein.

SARASTRO:
Lead these two strangers to our temple of
probation, and cover their heads for they
must first be purified.

Monostatos is led away by slaves.

SCHLUßCHOR:
Wenn Tugend und Gerechtigkeit
den großen Pfad mit Ruhm bestreut,
dann ist die Erd' ein Himmelreich,
und Sterbliche den Göttern gleich.

CHORUS:
When virtue and justice are humanity's
ultimate ideals, then earth is indeed heaven,
and mortal men are like gods!

Veils are placed over the heads of Tamino and Papageno.
Sarastro takes Pamina's hand and goes with her through the middle door.
Tamino and Papageno exit with two Priests.

ACT II – Scene 1

A palm grove in which all of the trees are silver with leaves of gold.
Sarastro and Priests enter.

SARASTRO:
Ihr, in dem Weisheitstempel eingeweihten Diener der großen Götter Osiris und Isis! Mit reiner Seele erklär' ich euch, daß unsre heutige Versammlung eine der wichtigsten unsrer Zeit ist.
Tamino, ein Königssohn, will ins Heiligtum des größten Lichtes blicken. Diesen Tugendhaften zu bewachten, ihm freundschaftlich die Hand zu bieten, sei heute eine unsrer wichtigsten Pflichten.

SARASTRO:
You, who are ordained in the Temple of Wisdom, are servants of the great gods: Osiris and Isis! With a pure heart I advise you, that our meeting today is the most important in our history.
Tamino, a king's son, will gaze into the sublime light of the sanctuary. Our most important duty today is to protect this virtuous youth, and to welcome him warmly.

ERSTER PRIESTER:
Er besitzt Tugend?

FIRST PRIEST:
Is he virtuous?

SARASTRO:
Tugend!

SARASTRO:
Most virtuous!

ZWEITER PRIESTER:
Auch Verschwiegenheit?

SECOND PRIEST:
Can he maintain his silence?

SARASTRO:
Verschwiegenheit!

SARASTRO:
He can!

DRITTER PRIESTER:
Ist wohltätig?

THIRD PRIEST:
Is he benevolent?

SARASTRO:
Wohltätig! Haltet ihr ihn für würdig, so folgt meinem Beispiele.

SARASTRO:
He is! If you believe he is worthy, then follow my example.

They blow three times on their horns.

Gerührt über die Einigkeit eurer Herzen, dankt Sarastro euch im Namen der Menschheit. Mag immer das Vorurteil seinen Tadel über uns Eingeweihte auslassen! Jedoch, das böse Vorurteil soll schwinden; und es wird schwinden, sobald Tamino selbst die Größe unserer schweren Kunst besitzen wird.

Sarastro is moved by the unanimity in your hearts, and thanks you in the name of all mankind. May Tamino never judge the deeds of the ordained! Any of his prejudices will disappear as soon as he becomes part of our brotherhood.

Pamina haben die Götter dem holden Jüngling bestimmt; dies ist der Grund, warum ich sie der stolzen Mutter entriß. Das Weib dünkt sich groß zu sein; hofft durch Blendwerk und Aberglauben das Volk zu berücken und unsern festen Tempelblau zu zerstören.

Pamina has been designated by the gods for this noble young man. That is why I kidnapped her from her haughty mother. That woman considers herself great, and hopes to beguile the populace through delusion and superstition, and to destroy the firm foundations of our temples.

Allein, das soll sie nicht. Tamino, der holde Jüngling, soll ihn mit uns befestigen und als Eingeweihter der Tugend Lohn, dem Laster aber Strafe sein.

However, she shall not succeed. Tamino himself shall become one of us, and aid us to strengthen the power of virtue and wisdom.

Three blasts on the horns are repeated.

SPRECHER:
Großer Sarastro, wird Tamino auch die harten Prüfungen, die seiner warten, bekämpfen? Verzeih, daß ich so frei bin, dir meinen Zweifel zu eröffnen! Mich bangt es um den Jüngling. Er ist Prinz!

SPEAKER:
Great Sarastro, will Tamino be able to overcome the difficult ordeals that await him? I apologize for being so forthright by expressing my doubts to you! I am worried for this young man. He is a prince!

SARASTRO:
Noch mehr! Er ist Mensch!

SARASTRO:
But more important than that, he is a man!

SPRECHER:
Wenn es nur aber in seiner frühen Jugend leblos erblaßte?

SPEAKER:
But what if he would die so young?

SARASTRO:
Dann ist er Osiris und Isis gegeben und wird der Götter Freuden früher fühlen als wir.

SARASTRO:
Then he will be given to Osiris and Isis and will experience their celestial joys sooner than we.

Three blasts on the horns are repeated.

Man führe Tamino mit seinem eisegefährten in den Vorhof des Tempels ein.

Let Tamino and his companion be led into the court of the temple.

(to the Priest)

Und du, Freund, vollziehe dein heiliges Amt und lehre sie die Macht der Götter erkennen!

And you my friend, fulfill your holy duty and teach them to recognize the might of the gods.

THE MAGIC FLUTE

O I - sis und O - si - ris, schenket der Weisheit Geist dem neu - en Paar!

SARASTRO:
O Isis und Osiris, schenket der Weisheit
Geist dem neuen Paar, die ihr der Wand'rer
Schritte lenket.
Stärkt mit Geduld sie in Gefahr.

CHOR:
Stärkt mit Geduld sie in Gefahr!

SARASTRO:
Laßt sie der Prüfung Früchte sehen;
Doch sollten sie zu Grabe gehen,
So lohnt der Tugend kühnen Lauf,
Nehmt sie in euren Wohnsitz auf.

CHOR:
Nehmt sie in euren Wohnsitz auf.

SARASTRO:
O Isis and Osiris, lead this faithful pair to the
path of wisdom! Concede your blessed
protection, strengthen their hearts and fortify
them with patience when they are in danger.

CHORUS:
Fortify them with patience when they are in
danger.

SARASTRO.
Grant that they bear the trial bravely, and
that their prayers are not denied. But if you
have fated them to fail, please take them,
and grant them life beyond the tomb.

CHORUS:
Grant them life beyond the tomb.

ACT II - Scene 2

The courtyard of the temple. It is night.
Tamino and Papageno are led in by the Speaker and the Second Priests.
Before departing, they remove the veils from Tamino and Papageno.

TAMINO:
Eine schreckliche Nacht! - Papageno, bist
du noch bei mir?

PAPAGENO:
Ja, freilich!

TAMINO:
Wo denkst du, dass wir uns nun befinden?

TAMINO:
What a horrible night! Papageno are you
still with me?

PAPAGENO:
I most certainly am!

TAMINO:
Where do you think we are now?

PAPAGENO:
Wo? Ja, wenn's nicht so finster wär, wollt' ich dir das schon sagen, aber so...
Oh!

O weh!

TAMINO:
Was ist's?

PAPAGENO:
Mir wird nicht wohl bei der Sache! Ich glaube, ich bekomme ein kleines Fieber.

TAMINO:
Pfui, Papageno! Sei ein Mann!

PAPAGENO:
Aber ich wollt', ich wär ein Mädchen!

O! o! o! Das ist mein letzter Augenblick!

PAPAGENO:
Where we are? Well if it were not so dark, I might be able to tell you, but this way ....
Oh!
(Thunder is heard)
Help!

TAMINO:
What is it?

PAPAGENO:
I don't feel comfortable in this situation! I have a feeling that ice-cold shivers are running up and down my spine.

TAMINO:
Shame on you Papageno, be a man!

PAPAGENO:
I wish I were a girl!
(Very loud thunder)
Oh! Oh! Oh! My last hour has come!

The Speaker, Priest, and the Second Priest return. All carry torches.

SPRECHER:
Ihr Fremdlinge, was sucht oder fordert ihr von uns? Was treibt euch an, in unsere Mauern zu dringen?

TAMINO:
Freundschaft und Liebe.

ÄLTERER PRIESTER:
Bist du bereit, sie mit deinem Leben zu erkämpfen?

TAMINO:
Ja!

SPRECHER:
Prinz, noch ist's Zeit zu weichen, einen Schritt weiter, und es ist zu spät.

SPEAKER:
What are you seeking, or asking from us? What is your reason for invading our sanctuary?

TAMINO:
Friendship and love.

ELDERLY PRIEST:
And are you prepared to sacrifice your life for friendship and love?

TAMINO:
I am!

SPEAKER:
Prince, there is still time to turn back. One step further and it's too late.

TAMINO:
Weisheitslehre sei mein Sieg; Pamina, das holde Mädchen, mein Lohn!

SPRECHER:
Du unterziehst dich jeder Prüfung dich?

TAMINO:
Jeder!

SPRECHER:
Reiche deine Hand mir!

ZWEITER PRIESTER:
Willst auch du dir Weisheitsliebe erkämpfen?

PAPAGENO:
Kämpfen ist meine Sache nicht. Ich verlang ja im Grunde auch gar keine Weisheit. Ich bin so ein Naturmensch, der sich mit Schlaf, Speise und Trank zufriedengibt. Und wenn es einmal sein könnte, daß ich mir ein hübsches Weibchen fange.

ZWEITER PRIESTER:
Die wirst du nie erhalten, wenn du dich nicht unseren Prüfungen unterziehst.

PAPAGENO:
Und worin bestehen diese Prüfungen?

ZWEITER PRIESTER:
Dich allen unseren Gesetzen zu unterwerfen, selbst den Tod nicht zu scheuen.

PAPAGENO:
Ich bleibe ledig!

ZWEITER PRIESTER:
Aber wenn du dir ein tugendhaftes, schönes Mädchen erwerben könntest?

PAPAGENO:
Ich bleibe ledig!

TAMINO:
Wisdom will be my victory, and the lovely Pamina my reward!

SPEAKER:
Are you willing to undergo each trial?

TAMINO:
Every one!

SPEAKER:
Give me your hand!
(They clasp hands)

SECOND PRIEST: *(to Papageno).*
Will you also fight for the love of wisdom?

PAPAGENO:
Fighting is not my business, and in principal, I really don't desire wisdom either. I am a son of nature, who is content with sleep, food, and drink. And if possible, I would like to find a pretty little wife.

SECOND PRIEST:
But you will never obtain one, if you do not submit to our trial.

PAPAGENO:
And what does this trial consist of?

SECOND PRIEST:
To surrender to all our laws, and not shrink from death.

PAPAGENO:
I'll remain single!

SECOND PRIEST:
But what if you could get a virtuous and beautiful young girl?

PAPAGENO:
I'll remain single!

ZWEITER PRIESTER:
Wenn nun aber Sarastro dir ein Mädchen aufbewahrt hätte, das an Farbe und Kleidung dir ganz gleich wäre?

PAPAGENO:
Mir ganz gleich? Ist sie jung?

ZWEITER PRIESTER:
Jung und schön!

PAPAGENO:
Und heißt?

ZWEITER PRIESTER:
Papagena.

PAPAGENO:
Wie? Papa...

ZWEITER PRIESTER:
Papagena.

PAPAGENO:
Papagena? Haha, die möcht ich aus bloßer Neugierde schon sehen.

ZWEITER PRIESTER:
Sehen kannst du sie!

PAPAGENO:
Aber wenn....Ich bleibe ledig!ich sie gesehen habe, hernach muß ich sterben?

ZWEITER PRIESTER:
Sehen kannst du sie, aber bis zur verlaufenen Zeit kein Wort mit ihr sprechen; wird dein Geist so viel Standhaftigkeit besitzen, deine Zunge in Schranken zu halten?

PAPAGENO:
O ja!

SPRECHER:
Deine Hand! Du sollst sie sehen.

SECOND PRIEST:
But what if Sarastro already has reserved a virtuous and pretty girl for you, one who is just like you?

PAPAGENO:
Just like me? Is she young?

SECOND PRIEST:
Young and beautiful!

PAPAGENO:
And what's her name?

SECOND PRIEST:
Papagena.

PAPAGENO:
What? Papa...

SECOND PRIEST:
Papagena.

PAPAGENO:
Papagena? Ha ha, and just out of curiosity, I'd like to see her.

SECOND PRIEST:
You can see her!

PAPAGENO:
But after... I remain single! But after I've seen her, must I die?
(Second Priest makes a sign of doubt.)

SECOND PRIEST:
You can see her, but in the meantime, you cannot speak to her. Will your mind be strong enough to control your tongue?

PAPAGENO:
Oh, yes!

SPEAKER:
Your hand! You shall see her!
(They clasp hands)

ÄLTERER PRIESTER:
Auch dir, Prinz, legen die Götter ein heilsames Stillschweigen auf; ohne dieses seid ihr beide verloren. Du wirst Pamina sehen, aber nie sie sprechen dürfen; dies ist der Anfang eurer Prüfungszeit.

BEIDE PRIESTER:
Bewahret euch vor Weibertücken: dies ist des Bundes erste Pflicht. Manch weiser Mann ließ sich berücken, er fehlte und versah sich's nicht. Verlassen sah er sich am Ende, vergolten seine Treu' mit Hohn. Vergebens rang er seine Hände, Tod und Verzweiflung war sein Lohn.

PAPAGENO:
He, Lichter her! Lichter her! Das ist doch wunderlich, so oft einen die Herrn verlassen, sieht man mit offenen Augen nichts.

TAMINO:
Ertrag es mit Geduld, und denke, es ist der Götter Wille.

ELDERLY PRIEST: *(to Tamino)*
The gods impose a holy silence on you too, my Prince. If you speak, both of you will be lost. You will see Pamina, but do not speak to her until the appointed hour. This the beginning of your trial.

BOTH PRIESTS:
Your first duty is to be aware of woman's treachery, because many men found themselves forsaken, led astray and ensnared by them. In the end man was all alone and his faithfulness was met with scorn. He wrung his hands in vain, for pain and death were his rewards.

(As it grows dark, both Priests leave)

PAPAGENO:
Hey! Lights please! It is really amazing. As soon as these gentlemen leave us, you can't see anything with your eyes open.

TAMINO:
Bear it patiently and remember that it is the will of Gods!

The Three Ladies rush in with torches.

DREI DAMEN:
Wie, wie, wie? Ihr an diesem Schreckensort? Nie, nie, nie! Kommt ihr wieder glücklich fort! Tamino, dir ist Tod geschworen! Du, Papageno, bist verloren!

PAPAGENO:
Nein, nein, das wär' zu viel.

TAMINO:
Papageno, schweige still! Willst du dein Gelübde brechen, nicht mit Weibern hier zu sprechen?

THE THREE LADIES:
What, what, what? You in this place of terror? Never, never, never! Get safely out of here! Tamino, you are destined to die! Papageno, you are lost!

PAPAGENO:
No, no, no, that would be too much!

TAMINO:
Papageno, please be quiet! Do you want to break your oath never to speak to women?

PAPAGENO:
Du hörst ja, wir sind beide hin.

TAMINO:
Stille, sag ich, schweige still!

PAPAGENO:
Immer still, und immer still!

DREI DAMEN:
Ganz nah' ist euch die Königin!
Sie drang im Tempel heimlich ein.

PAPAGENO:
Wie? Was? Sie soll im Tempel sein?

TAMINO:
Stille, sag' ich, schweige still! Wirst du
immer so vermessen deiner Eidespflicht
vergessen?

DREI DAMEN:
Tamino, hör'! Du bist verloren!
Gedenke an die Königin!
Man zischelt viel sich in die Ohren von
dieser Priester falschem Sinn.

TAMINO:
Ein Weiser prüft und achtet nicht,
Was der gemeine Pöbel spricht.

DREI DAMEN:
Man zischelt viel sich in die Ohren
Von dieser Priester falschem Sinn.
Man sagt, wer ihrem Bunde schwört,
Der fährt zur Höll' mit Haut und Haar.

PAPAGENO:
Das wär', beim Teufel, unerhört!
Sag' an, Tamino, ist das wahr?

TAMINO:
Geschwätz, von Weibern nachgesagt,
Von Heuchlern aber ausgedacht.

PAPAGENO:
Doch sagt es auch die Königin.

PAPAGENO:
You heard it, we're both lost!

TAMINO:
Quiet, I tell you! Please don't talk!

PAPAGENO:
All you say is quiet and don't talk!

THE THREE LADIES:
The Queen is very close by, since she has
secretly entered the temple.

PAPAGENO:
How? What? She's in the temple?

TAMINO:
Quiet, I tell you, don't talk! Will you ever
be so bold to forget the oath you have
sworn?

THE THREE LADIES:
Tamino, listen! You are lost!
Think of the Queen.
Around here, the Priests are whispering
many falsehoods about her.

TAMINO: *(to himself)*
A wise man pays no attention to the talk of
evil people.

THE THREE LADIES:
It's been said that these Priests have
nothing good in mind.
They say that those who join the order are
condemned to hell!

PAPAGENO:
That's outrageous!
Tell me, Tamino, is it true?

TAMINO:
That's nonsense invented by bigots and
repeated by women!

PAPAGENO:
Yet the Queen has said it too.

TAMINO:
Sie ist ein Weib, hat Weibersinn.
Sei still, mein Wort sei dir genug:
Denk' deiner Pflicht und handle klug.

DREI DAMEN:
Warum bist du mit uns so spröde?

Auch Papageno schweigt...so rede!

PAPAGENO:
Ich möchte gerne, woll...

TAMINO:
Still!

PAPAGENO:
Ihr seht, daß ich nicht kann das Plaudern
lassen, ist wahrlich eine Schand' für mich!

TAMINO:
Daß du nicht kannst das Plaudern lassen,
ist wahrlich eine Schand' für dich!

DREI DAMEN:
Wir/Sie müßen sie/uns mit Scham
verlassen, es plaudert keiner sicherlich.

TAMINO, PAPAGENO:
Von festem Geiste ist ein Mann,
er denket, was er sprechen kann.

TAMINO:
She's just like all women.
Take my word for it and hold your tongue.
Think of your duty and be smart!

THE THREE LADIES: *(to Tamino)*
Why are you so cold and callous?

(Tamino intimates to them that he is not allowed to speak.)
And Papageno also doesn't talk! Speak!

PAPAGENO: *(aside to the Ladies).*
I would li.......

TAMINO:
Be quiet!

PAPAGENO: *(aside to the Ladies)*
You see that the fact I can't stop talking is
really a disgrace!

TAMINO:
The fact that you can't stop talking is really
a disgrace!

THREE LADIES:
We're humiliated and better leave them
now because no one is talking to us.

TAMINO, PAPAGENO:
The man who thinks before he speaks
certainly has sound judgment.

As the Three Ladies are about to go, the Priests are heard from inside the Temple.

PRIESTERS:
Entweiht ist die heilige Schwelle!
Hinab mit den Weibern zur Hölle!

CHORUS OF PRIESTS:
The sacred threshold is defiled!
Condemn the women to death and damnation!

(Thunder and lightning)

DREI DAMEN:
O weh! O weh! O weh!

THE THREE LADIES: *(rushing away)*
Oh what misery and grief!

PAPAGENO:
O weh, o weh, o weh!

PAPAGENO: *(falls down in fright)*
Oh what misery and grief!

The Priests enter carrying torches.

SPRECHER:
Heil dir, Jüngling! Dein standhaft männliches Betragen hat gesiegt. Wir wollen also mit reinem Herzen unsere Wanderschaft weiter fortsetzen.

So! Nun komm!

SPEAKER:
Hail young man! Your steadfast, manly behavior has won a victory! Therefore, because of your virtue, we wish to continue our travels.
(The Priest veils Tamino)
Come then!

The Priest and Tamino leave.

ZWEITER PRIESTER:
Was seh ich, Freund! Stehe auf! Wie ist dir?

SECOND PRIEST:
What do I see my friend? Get up! What has happened to you?

PAPAGENO:
Ich lieg' in einer Ohnmacht!

PAPAGENO:
I'm lying here helpless!

ZWEITER PRIESTER:
Auf! Sammle dich, und sei ein Mann!

SECOND PRIEST:
Get up! Get yourself together and be a man!

PAPAGENO:
Aber sagt mir nur, meine lieben Herren, warum muß ich denn alle diese Qualen und Schrecken empfinden? Wenn mir ja die Götter eine Papagena bestimmten, warum denn mit so viel Gefahren sie erringen?

PAPAGENO:
But tell me, my dear gentlemen, why do I have to be subjected to all these torments and horrors? If the gods really have destined a Papagena for me, why do I have to endanger myself to win her?

ZWEITER PRIESTER:
Diese neugierige Frage mag deine vernunft dir beantworten. Komm! Meine Pflicht ist allein, dich weiterzuführen.

SECOND PRIEST:
Let your own reason answer your own inquisitive question. Come, my only duty is to lead you forward..

The Priest covers Papageno's head with a veil.

PAPAGENO:
Bei so einer ewigen Wanderschaft, da möcht' einem wohl die Liebe auf immer vergehen.

PAPAGENO:
If I have to wander like this, I'd prefer to give up love forever.

Papageno leaves with the Second Priest.

THE MAGIC FLUTE

ACT II – SCENE 3

A Garden. Pamina sleeps, the moon shining on her face. Monostatos arrives.

MONOSTATOS:
Ha, da find' ich ja die spröde Schöne!
Welcher Mensch würde bei so einem
Anblick kalt und unempfindlich bleiben?

Das Feuer, das in mir glimmt, wird mich
noch verzehren! Wenn ich wüßte - daß ich
so ganz allein und unbelauscht wäre - ich
wagte es noch einmal.

Das Mädchen wird noch um meinen
Verstand mich bringen.Es ist doch eine
verdammte närrische Sache um die Liebe!
Ein Küßchen, dächte ich, ließe sich
entschuldigen.

MONOSTATOS:
Ah, here is the delicate beauty. What
human being could remain cold and
insensitive to such a vision?

The fire that burns within me will consume
me yet! If I only knew that I was alone and
that no one was looking, I'd dare one more
time.

This girl will make me lose my mind yet.
Love is such a crazy thing. I would think a
little kiss would be excusable.

Allegro
MONOSTATOS

Al - les fühlt der Lie - be Freuden, schnäbelt, tändelt, herzt und küsst.

Alles fühlt der Liebe Freuden, schnäbelt,
tändelt, herzt und küßt; Und ich sollt' die Liebe
meiden, Weil ein Schwarzer häßlich ist!

Ist mir denn kein Herz gegeben? Bin ich
nicht von Fleisch und Blut? Immer ohne
Weibchen leben, Wäre wahrlich Höllenglut!

Drum so will ich, weil ich lebe,
Schnäbeln, küssen, zärtlich sein!
Lieber guter Mond, vergebe,
Eine Weiße nahm mich ein.
Weiß ist schön! Ich muß sie küssen;
Mond, verstecke dich dazu!
Sollt' es dich zu sehr verdrießen,
O so mach' die Augen zu!

Everybody enjoys love with its caresses and
embraces, and I'm supposed to
relinquish love because my skin is dark.

Don't I have a heart within me? Am I not
made of flesh and blood? It is pure hell to
have to live without a woman.

That's why, while I'm still alive, I want
kisses and tenderness.
Dear good moon, please forgive me,
because a white maiden has enticed me.
Her white skin is beautiful, and I must kiss
her. Moon, hide yourself for a moment, and
if it disturbs your bliss, then close your
eyes!

*As Monostatos creeps toward Pamina,
the Queen suddenly appears amid thunder and lightning.*

KÖNIGIN:
Zurück!

QUEEN: *(to Monostatos)*
Go back!

PAMINA:
Ihr Götter!

PAMINA: *(Pamina awakens)*
Oh Gods!

MONOSTATOS:
O weh! Das ist...die Göttin der Nacht!

MONOSTATOS: *(backing away)*
What's this...the Queen of the Night!

PAMINA:
Mutter! Mutter! Meine Mutter!

PAMINA: *(arising)*
Mother, mother, my mother!
(She falls into her mother's arms.)

MONOSTATOS:
Mutter? Hm, das muß man von weitem belauschen.

MONOSTATOS:
Mother? Hm, I ought to spy on them from a distance.
(Monostatos leaves)

KÖNIGIN:
Wo ist der Jüngling, den ich an dich sandte?

QUEEN:
Where is the young man I had sent to you?

PAMINA:
Er hat sich den Eingeweihten gewidmet.

PAMINA:
He has devoted himself to the order.

KÖNIGIN:
Unglückliche Tochter, nun bist du auf ewig mir entrissen.

QUEEN:
Oh my unfortunate daughter. Now you will be forever stolen from me.

PAMINA:
Entrissen? O fliehen wir, liebe Mutter! Unter deinem Schutz trotz' ich jeder Gefahr.

PAMINA:
Stolen? Oh let's escape, dear mother! With your protection, I'll venture every danger.

KÖNIGIN:
Schutz? Liebes Kind, deine Mutter kann dich nicht mehr schützen. Mit deines Vaters Tod ging meine Macht zu Grabe. Übergab freiwillig den siebenfachen Sonnenkreis den Eingeweihten; diesen mächtigen Sonnenkreis trägt Sarastro auf seiner Brust.

QUEEN:
Protection? My dear child, your mother can no longer protect you. With your father's death, my power disappeared because I willfully surrendered the seven-sided sun shield, the powerful zodiax which Sarastro know wears on his chest.

The Queen draws out a dagger.

THE MAGIC FLUTE

Siehst du hier diesen Stahl? Er ist für Sarastro geschliffen. Du wirst ihn töten und den mächtigen Sonnenkreis mir überliefern.

PAMINA:
Aber, liebste Mutter!....

KÖNIGIN:
Kein Wort!

Do you see this dagger? It has been sharpened for Sarastro. You will kill him, seize the powerful zodiac, and bring it back to me.

(She forces Pamina to take the dagger)
PAMINA:
But, dearest mother!....

QUEEN:
Not a word!

Allegro assai
QUEEN OF THE NIGHT

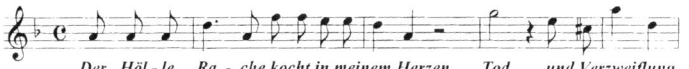

Der Höl - le Ra - che kocht in meinem Herzen, Tod und Verzweiflung,

Der Hölle Rache kocht in meinem Herzen,
Tod und Verzweiflung, flammet um mich her!

Fühlt nicht durch dich Sarastro
Todesschmerzen, so bist du meine Tochter
nimmermehr. Verstoßen sei auf ewig,
verlassen sei auf ewig.

Zertrümmert sei'n auf ewig alle Bande der
Natur, Wenn nicht durch dich Sarastro wird
erblassen!
Hört, Rachegötter, hört der Mutter Schwur!

Hell's revenge is raging in my heart.
Death and despair wildly flame around!

Go forth, and bear my vengeance to
Sarastro, or as my daughter, you shall be
disowned, and be forever rejected and
forsaken.

Our natural bond will be destroyed forever
if you do not kill Sarastro!
Hear, gods of vengeance, hear a mother's
curse!

(The Queen disappears amidst thunder)

PAMINA:
Morden soll ich? Götter, das kann ich
nicht! Götter, was soll ich tun?

MONOSTATOS:
Dich mir anvertrauen.

PAMINA:
Ha!

MONOSTATOS:
Warum zitterst du? Vor meiner schwarzen
Farbe, oder vor dem ausgedachten Mord?

PAMINA: *(with dagger in hand).*
I must kill someone? Gods, I can't do that!
Gods, what shall I do?

MONOSTATOS: *(taking her dagger).*
Trust me.

PAMINA: *(frightened).*
Ha!

MONOSTATOS:
Why do you tremble? Is it because of my black
skin or because you have murderous intensions?

PAMINA:
Du weißt also?

MONOSTATOS:
Alles. Du hast also nur einen Weg, dich und deine Mutter zu retten.

PAMINA:
Der wäre?

MONOSTATOS:
Mich zu lieben! Ja oder nein?

PAMINA:
Nein!

MONOSTATOS:
Nein? Liebe oder Tod!

PAMINA:
Nien!

MONOSTATOS:
Nein?

PAMINA: *(timidly).*
Then you know?

MONOSTATOS:
I know everything. There is only one way to save yourself and your mother.

PAMINA:
Which is?

MONOSTATOS:
To love me! Yes or no?

PAMINA: *(trembling)*
No!

MONOSTATOS: *(angrily)*
No? Love or death!

PAMINA: *(decidedly)*
No!

MONOSTATOS:
No?

Sarastro comes between them, raises a threatening arm, and hurls Monostatos back.

MONOSTATOS:

So fahre denn hin! Herr, man hat deinen Tod geschworen, darum wollt' ich dich rächen.

SARASTRO:
Ich weiß nur allzuviel. Ich weiß, daß deine Seele ebenso schwarz als dein Gesicht ist. Geh!

MONOSTATOS:
Jetzt such' ich die Mutter auf, weil mir die Tochter nicht beschieden ist.

PAMINA:
Herr, strafe meine Mutter nicht! Der Schmerz über meine Abwesenheit...

MONOSTATOS:
(raises the dagger, and then falls before Sarastro)
I am not guilty! Sir, since they swore to kill you, I sought revenge for you.

SARASTRO:
I know enough. I know that your soul is as dark as your face. Go!

MONOSTATOS: *(as he leaves)*
Since the daughter is not meant for me, I'll conspire with the mother.
(Monostatos leaves)

PAMINA:
Sir, do not punish my mother! Her sorrow due to my absence...

SARASTRO::
Ich weiß alles. Weiß, daß sie in unterirdischen Gemächern des Tempels herumirrt und Rache über mich und die Menschheit kocht; allein, du sollst sehen, wie ich mich an deiner Mutter räche.

SARASTRO:
I know everything. I know that she is roaming between the walls of the temple, seeking revenge on me and mankind. But, I will show you how I take vengeance upon your mother.

Larghetto
SARASTRO

In die - sen heil - gen Hallen kennt man die Ra - che nicht,

In diesen heilgen Hallen Kennt man die Rache nicht, und ist ein Mensch gefallen, Führt Liebe ihn zur Pflicht. Dann wandelt er an Freundes Hand vergnügt und froh in's bess're Land.

Within these sacred walls, revenge and sorrow do not exist. When a man has failed, only love will guide him to do his duty. Then he'll walk happily to a better life, guided by the hand of friendship.

In diesen heil'gen Mauern, wo Mensch den Menschen liebt, kann kein Verräter lauern, weil man dem Feind vergibt.
Wen solche Lehren nicht erfreun, verdienet nicht ein Mensch zu sein.

Within these sacred walls, where man loves his fellow man, there is no treachery, because enemies are forgiven. Whoever does not appreciate this knowledge, does not deserve to walk this earth.

Pamina and Sarastro exit.

ACT II - Scene 4

A hall in the Temple of Probation.
Tamino and Papageno, unveiled, are led in by the two Priests.

SPRECHER:
Hier seid ihr euch beide allein überlassen. Sobald die Posaune tönt, dann nehmt ihr euren Weg dahin. Prinz, lebt wohl! Noch einmal, vergeßt das Wort nicht: Schweigen.

SPEAKER:
You are on your own but dependent upon each other. As soon as you hear the sound of the trumpet, start on your way. Farewell, Prince. Once more, don't forget, you are committed to silence.
(The Priest exits)

ZWEITER PRIESTER:
Papageno, wer an diesem Ort sein Stillschweigen bricht, den strafen die Götter durch Donner und Blitz. Leb wohl!

SECOND PRIEST:
Papageno, anyone who breaks his silence in this palace is punished by the gods with thunder and lightning. Farewell.
(The Second Priest exits)

PAPAGENO:
Tamino!

PAPAGENO:
Tamino!

TAMINO:
St!

TAMINO:
Ssh!

PAPAGENO:
Das ist ein lustiges Leben! Wär' ich lieber in meiner Strohhütte, oder im Wald, da hör ich doch noch manchmal einen Vogel pfeifen.

PAPAGENO:
What a jolly life this is! I'd rather be in my straw hut or in the woods; at least there I'd hear a bird singing once in a while.

TAMINO:
St!

TAMINO:
Ssh!

PAPAGENO:
Also, mit mir selber werd ich ja vielleicht noch reden dürfen; und auch wir zwei, wir können miteinander sprechen, wir sind ja Männer. La la la-la la la!

PAPAGENO:
Well, at least I'm allowed to talk to myself! And of course, the two of us can talk to each other, because we are men! La la la-la la la!

TAMINO:
St!

TAMINO: *(reprimanding him)*
Ssh!

PAPAGENO:
Nicht einmal einen Tropfen Wasser bekommt man bei diesen Leuten; viel weniger sonst was.

PAPAGENO:
One doesn't even get a single drop of water from these people, let alone anything else.

THE MAGIC FLUTE

An old, ugly woman appears, bearing a large cup of water.
Papageno stares at her for a long time.

Ist das für mich?

Is that for me?

ALTES WEIB:
Ja, mein Engel!

OLD WOMAN:
Yes my angel!

PAPAGENO:
Wasser! Nicht mehr und nicht weniger als Wasser. Sag du mir, du unbekannte Schöne, werden alle fremden Gäste auf diese Art bewirtet?

PAPAGENO: *(he drinks)*
Water! Nothing more or less than water. Tell me, unknown beauty, are all foreign guests treated this way?

ALTES WEIB:
Freilich, mein Engel!

OLD WOMAN:
Surely my angel!

PAPAGENO:
So, so! Auf diese Art werden die Fremden auch nicht gar zu häufig kommen.

PAPAGENO:
Is that so? In that case, I guess the foreigners don't come too frequently.

ALTES WEIB:
Sehr wenig.

OLD WOMAN:
Very seldom.

PAPAGENO:
Das kann ich mir denken. Geh, komm, Alte, setze dich ein bisser! Her zu mir, mir ist die Zeit verdammt lang.
Sag du mir, wie alt bist denn du?

PAPAGENO:
That's what I thought. Come, old woman, sit down next to me for a while. I feel terribly bored here. *(She sits down by his side)*
Tell me how old you are?

ALTES WEIB:
Wie alt?

OLD WOMAN:
How old?

PAPAGENO:
Ja!

PAPAGENO:
Yes!

ALTES WEIB:
Achtzehn Jahr und zwei Minuten.

OLD WOMAN:
Eighteen years and two minutes.

PAPAGENO:
Achtzig Jahr?

PAPAGENO:
You're eighty?

ALTES WEIB:
Achtzehn Jahr und zwei Minuten.

OLD WOMAN:
Eighteen years and two minutes.

PAPAGENO:
Achtzehn Jahr und zwei Minuten?

ALTES WEIB:
Ja!

PAPAGENO:
Ha ha ha! Ei, du junger Engel! Sag mal, hast du auch einen Geliebten?

ALTES WEIB:
Ei, freilich, mein Engel!

PAPAGENO:
Ist er auch so jung wie du?

ALTES WEIB:
Nicht gar, er ist um zehn Jahre älter.

PAPAGENO:
Was, um zehn Jahre ist der noch älter als du? Das muß ja eine feurige Liebe sein! Und wie nennt sich denn dein Liebhaber?

ALTES WEIB:
Papageno!

PAPAGENO:
Papageno? Wo ist er denn, dieser Papageno?

ALTES WEIB:
Da sitzt er, mein Engel!

PAPAGENO:
Was, ich wär dein Geliebter?

ALTES WEIB:
Ja, mein Engel!

PAPAGENO:
Sag du mir, wie heißt du denn?

ALTES WEIB:
Ich heiße....

PAPAGENO:
Eighteen years and two minutes?

OLD WOMAN:
Yes!

PAPAGENO:
Ha ha ha! You're really a very young angel! Tell me, do you have a sweetheart?

OLD WOMAN:
Of course, my angel!

PAPAGENO:
Is he as young as you are?

OLD WOMAN:
Not quite. He's ten years older.

PAPAGENO:
Ten year older than you are? That must be quite a passionate love! What's your sweetheart's name?

OLD WOMAN:
Papageno!

(Papageno falls from his seat)
PAPAGENO:
Papageno? Where is he then, this Papageno?

OLD WOMAN:
Her is sitting right there!

PAPAGENO:
What! I'm your sweetheart?

OLD WOMAN:
Yes my angel!

PAPAGENO:
Tell me. What is your name?

OLD WOMAN:
My name is....

THE MAGIC FLUTE

At the sound of loud thunder, the woman hobbles away.

PAPAGENO:
Oh!

PAPAGENO:
Oh!

Tamino shakes a warning finger at Papageno.

Nun sprech' ich aber kein Wort mehr!

From now on I won't speak another word!

The Three Youths bring a flute and bells.

DREI KNABEN:
Seid uns zum zweitenmal willkommen,
ihr Männer, in Sarastros Reich,
er schickt, was man euch abgenommen,
die Flöte und die Glöckchen euch.

THE THREE YOUTHS:
For the second time we welcome you to
Sarastro's kingdom. Sarastro is returning
what was taken from you: your flute and
the little bells.

A golden table covered with food and drink is unveiled.

Wollt ihr die Speisen nicht verschmähen,
so esset, trinket froh davon.
Wenn wir zum drittenmal uns sehen,
ist Freude eures Mutes Lohn.
Tamino, Mut! Nah ist das Ziel.
Du, Papageno, schweige still!

If you like the food on the table,
then drink and eat as much as you want.
When we will see each other for a third
time, it will be to celebrate your courage.
Tamino, courage, your goal is near.
And you Papageno, don't talk!

They present the flute to Tamino, the bells to Papageno, and then leave.

PAPAGENO:
Tamino, wollen wir nicht speisen?

Blase du nur fort auf deiner Flöte, ich will
meine Brocken blasen.

Herr Sarastro führt eine gute Küche. Auf
die Art, ja, da will ich schon schweigen,
wenn ich immer solche gute Bissen
bekomme. Nun, ich will sehen, ob auch der
Keller so gut bestellt ist.

Ha! Das ist Götterwein!

PAPAGENO:
Tamino, shall we eat?
(Tamino plays his flute)
You just play your flute and I'll play my
own game and eat.

(Papageno goes to the table and eats.)
That Mister Sarastro has a good cook!
With such delicious food, I don't mind
being silent. Now I'll see if his wine cellar
is as good as his kitchen.

(He fills his glass and drinks.)
Ha, this is wine fit for the gods!

As Pamina rushes in, Tamino stops playing his flute.

PAMINA:
Du hier? Gütige Götter! Dank euch! Ich hörte deine Flöte und so lief ich pfeilschnell dem Tone nach.
Aber du bist traurig? Sprichst nicht eine Silbe mit deiner Pamina?

TAMINO:
Ah!

PAMINA:
Ich soll dich meiden? Ich soll dich fliehen, ohne zu wissen, warum? Tamino, liebst du mich nicht mehr?
Papageno, sage du mir, sag, was ist meinem Freund?

PAPAGENO:
Hm, hm, hm.

PAMINA: *(happily).*
You're here? Good gods, I thank you! I heard the tones of your flute and rushed toward the sounds.
But you are sad? Don't you even say a word to your Pamina?

TAMINO:
Ah!
(indicating that she should leave)

PAMINA:
You want me to ignore you? I should leave you without knowing why? Tamino, don't you love me anymore?
Papageno, tell me what's the matter with my friend?

PAPAGENO:
(with full mouth, motions her to leave)
Hm, hm, hm.

Andante
PAMINA

Ach, ich fühl's es ist verschwunden, e - wig hin mein ganzes Glück.

PAMINA:
Ach, ich fühl's es ist verschwunden,
ewig hin der Liebe Glück!
Nimmer kommt ihr Wonnestunden
Meinem Herzen mehr zurück!
Sieh', Tamino, diese Tränen,
Fließen, Trauter, dir allein!
Fühlst du nicht der Liebe Sehnen,
So wird Ruh' im Tode sein!

PAPAGENO:
Nicht wahr, Tamino, ich kann auch schweigen, wenn's sein muß.
Ja; bei so einem Unternehmen, da bin ich ein Mann.

Der Koch und der Kellermeister sollen leben!

PAMINA:
Oh, I feel that the happiness of love is gone forever!
I will never feel joy and happiness again in my heart.
Look, Tamino, these tears flow just for you!
If you no longer love me, I'd rather die!

(Pamina leaves sadly)

PAPAGENO: *(eats hastily)*
You see, Tamino, I too can keep quiet when it is necessary.
If I have to, I am a man.

(Papageno drinks)
Long live the cook and the winemaster!

Three trumpet calls are heard, and Tamino indicates that Papageno should leave.

Geh du nur voraus, ich komm dann schon nach.	You go first, and then I'll follow.
	(Tamino pushes Papageno to leave)
Nein! Der Stärkere bleibt da!	No! The stronger one stays here!
	(The three trumpet calls sound)
Aha, das geht uns an.	Aha, that concerns us.
Wir kommen schon. Aber hör mal, Tamino, was wird denn noch alles mit uns werden?	We're coming. But tell me Tamino, what's going to happen to us?
	(Tamino points upwards)
Ach, du meinst, die Götter soll ich fragen?	Do you mean that I should ask the gods?
	(Tamino indicates yes)
Ja, die könnten uns freilich mehr sagen, als wir wissen!	Yes, they surely can tell us more than we know!
	(The three calls are heard again)
Wile nur nicht so, wir kommen noch immer zeitlich genug, um uns braten zu lassen.	Don't hurry so much. We'll be in time to be roasted.

Tamino drags Papageno away forcefully.

ACT II - Scene 5

Interior vaults of the pyramid.

CHOR DER PRIESTER:
O Isis und Osiris, welche Wonne!
Die düst're Nacht verscheucht der Glanz der Sonne.
Bald fühlt der edle Jüngling neues Leben:
Bald ist er unserm Dienste ganz ergeben.
Sein Geist ist kühn, sein Herz ist rein,
Bald wird er unser würdig sein.

CHORUS OF THE PRIESTS:
Oh Isis and Osiris, what joy!
The dark night is chased away by the power of our sun.
Soon the noble youth will feel new life.
Soon he will be in our service and enlightened.
His spirit is brave; his heart is pure.
Soon he will be worthy of us.

(Tamino is brought in)

SARASTRO:
Prinz, dein Betragen war bis hierher männlich und gelassen; nun hast du noch zwei gefährliche Wege zu wandern. Schlägt dein Herz noch ebenso warm für Pamina, und wünschest du einst als ein weiser Fürst zu regieren, so mögen die Götter dich ferner begleiten.

Deine Hand! Man bringe Pamina!

SARASTRO:
Prince, until now your behavior has been manly and composed. But you still have two obstacles to overcome.
If you heart still beats warmly for Pamina, and you wish to reign with wisdom in the future, may the gods guide you.

Give me your hand! Bring Pamina here!

Two Priests go out and return with Pamina, who is veiled.

PAMINA:
Wo bin ich? Welch eine fürchterliche Stille! Wo ist Tamino?

PAMINA:
Where am I? How terribly quiet it is here? Where is Tamino?

SARASTRO:
Er wartet deiner, um dir das letzte Lebewohl zu sagen.

SARASTRO:
He awaits you, to bid you a last farewell.

PAMINA:
Das letzte Lebewohl? O wo ist er?

PAMINA:
A last farewell? Where is he?

SARASTRO:
Hier!

SARASTRO:
Here!

PAMINA:
Tamino!

PAMINA:
Tamino!

TAMINO:
Zurück!

PAMINA:
Soll ich dich, Teurer, nicht mehr seh'n?

SARASTRO:
Ihr werdet froh euch wiedersehn!

PAMINA:
Dein warten tödliche Gefahren!

TAMINO:
Die Götter mögen mich bewahren!

PAMINA:
Dein warten tödliche Gefahren!

TAMINO, SARASTRO:
Die Götter mögen mich/ihn bewahren!

PAMINA:
Du wirst dem Tode nicht entgehen,
Mir flüstert dieses Ahnung ein.

TAMINO, SARASTRO:
Der Götter Wille mag geschehen,
ihr Wink soll mir/ihm Gesetze sein!

PAMINA:
O liebtest du, wie ich dich liebe,
Du würdest nicht so ruhig sein.

TAMINO, SARASTRO:
Glaub mir, ich/er fühle/fühlet gleiche Triebe,
Werd'/Wird ewig dein Getreuer sein.

SARASTRO:
Die Stunde schlägt, nun müßt ihr scheiden!

PAMINA, TAMINO:
Wie bitter sind der Trennung Leiden!

SARASTRO:
Tamino muß nun wieder fort.

TAMINO:
Go back!

PAMINA:
My dear one, will I never see you again?

SARASTRO:
You surely will happily see each other again!

PAMINA:
Deadly dangers await you!

TAMINO:
May the gods protect me!

PAMINA.
Deadly dangers await you!

TAMINO, SARASTRO:
May the gods protect me/him!

PAMINA:
I have the feeling that you will not escape
death.

TAMINO, SARASTRO:
May the will of the gods be done,
and their desire be law for me/him.

PAMINA:
Oh if you loved me as I loved you, then you
surely would not be so calm.

TAMINO, SARASTRO:
Trust me, I/ he loves you with equal
passion, and I/he will love you forever.

SARASTRO:
The hour has come for you to separate!

PAMINA, TAMINO:
How bitter are the pains of separating!

SARASTRO:
Tamino must leave now.

TAMINO:
Pamina, ich muß wirklich fort!

PAMINA:
Tamino muß nun wirklich fort?

SARASTRO:
Nun muß er fort!

TAMINO:
Nun muß ich fort.

PAMINA:
So mußt du fort!

TAMINO:
Pamina, lebe wohl!

PAMINA:
Tamino, lebe wohl!

SARASTRO:
Nun eile fort. Dich ruft dein Wort.
Die Stunde schlägt, wir sehn uns wieder!

TAMINO, PAMINA:
Ach, gold'ne Ruhe, kehre wieder!
Lebe wohl! Lebe wohl!

TAMINO:
Pamina, I really must leave!

PAMINA:
Must Tamino really leave now?

SARASTRO:
Yes, he must leave now!

TAMINO:
Yes, I must leave now!

SARASTRO:
Then you must leave!

TAMINO:
Pamina, farewell!

PAMINA:
Tamino, farewell!

SARASTRO:
Now hurry. Your duty calls you. At the right time, we'll meet again!

TAMINO, PAMINA:
Oh, may peace return again!
Farewell! Farewell!

Pamina is led away by two Priests. Sarastro leaves with Tamino.

ACT II – Scene 6

A small garden.

PAPAGENO:
Tamino! Tamino! Willst du mich denn gänzlich verlassen?

Wenn ich nur wenigstens wüßte, wo ich wäre. Tamino! Tamino, solang ich lebe, geh' ich nicht mehr von dir! Aber dies einmal verlaß mich armen Reisegefährten nicht!

PAPAGENO: *(from outside)*
Tamino! Tamino! Are you leaving me all alone?

(looking around)
If I only knew where I was!
Tamino! Tamino, as long as I live I'll never leave you! Just this once don't desert your poor fellow traveller!

He reaches the door through which Tamino was led away.

EINE STIMME:
Zurück!

VOICE:
Go back!

PAPAGENO:
Barmherzige Götter! Wo wend' ich mich hin! Wenn ich nur wüßte, wo ich hereinkam. Tamino!

PAPAGENO:
Merciful Gods! Where shall I turn? If I only knew where I came in.
Tamino!

DIE STIMME:
Zurück!

THE VOICE:
Go back!

(Thunder and flames burst from the door)

PAPAGENO:
Nun kann ich weder vorwärts noch zurück!

Und muß am Ende gar verhungern. Geschieht mir schon recht! Warum bin ich denn auch mitgereist?

PAPAGENO:
Now I can't go either forwards or backwards!
(he cries)
And I'll have to starve here.
Serves me right! Why did I go along with him?

The Speaker, bearing a torch, approaches Papageno.

SPRECHER:
Mensch! Du hättest verdient, auf immer in finsteren Klüften der Erde zu wandern; die gütigen Götter aber entlassen dich der Strafe dich. Dafür aber wirst du das himmlische Vergnügen der Eingeweihten nie fühlen.

SPEAKER:
Man, you deserve to wander forever in the dark recesses of the earth, but the merciful gods exempt you from this punishment. However, you shall never experience the heavenly pleasures of the ordained.

PAPAGENO:
Je nun, es gibt ja noch andere Leute meinesgleichen! Mir wäre jetzt ein gutes Glas Wein das größte Vergnügen.

ÄLTERER PRIESTER:
Sonst hast du keinen Wunsch in dieser Welt?

PAPAGENO:
Bis jetzt nicht.

SPRECHER:
Man wird dich damit bedienen!

PAPAGENO:
So what, there are many people like me in the world. At the moment, I'd like nothing better than a good glass of wine.

ELDERLY PRIEST:
Otherwise, you have no other wish in this world?

PAPAGENO:
So far, no other wish.

SPEAKER:
It will be coming to you!

After the Priest exits, a large jug filled with wine emerges..

PAPAGENO:
Ach! Da ist er ja schon!

Herrlich! Himmlisch! Göttlich! Ha! Ich bin jetzt so vergnügt, daß ich bis zur Sonne fliegen könnte, wenn ich Flügel hätte! Ha! Mir wird so wunderlich ums Herz! Ich möchte... ich wünschte... ja, was denn?

PAPAGENO:
Hurray! There it is already!
(He drinks)
Delicious! Heavenly! Divine! Ha! I'm so delighted now that if I had wings, I could fly to the sun. Ha! I'm starting to feel so wonderful! I'd love...I'd wish...... but what?

Papageno plays the Glockenspiel.

Ein Mädchen oder Weibchen
wünscht Papageno sich!
O so ein sanftes Täubchen
wär' Seligkeit für mich!

Dann schmeckte mir Trinken und Essen,
dann könnt' ich mit Fürsten mich messen,
Des Lebens als Weiser mich freun,
und wie im Elysium sein!

A girl or a little wife is what Papageno would love to have!
Oh such a gentle turtledove would be pure heaven!

Then I'd love to drink and eat,
and measure up to royalty.
I'd enjoy life like a wise man, and feel I had arrived in Elysium!

Ach, kann ich denn keiner von allen den reizenden Mädchen gefallen? Helf' eine mir nur aus der Not, sonst gräm' ich mich wahrlich zu Tod! Wird keine mir Liebe gewähren, So muß mich die Flamme verzehren! Doch küßt mich ein weiblicher Mund, So bin ich schon wieder gesund!	Oh, doesn't any fair maiden want me? Someone please liberate me from my misery, or else I'll cry myself to death! If no young girl gives her love to me, I'll be consumed by flames! However, if I should receive a woman's kiss, I'd be in heavenly bliss!

The old woman, leaning on her cane, happily arrives.

ALTES WEIB:
Da bin ich schon, mein Engel!

OLD WOMAN:
Here I am, my angel!

PAPAGENO:
Was, du hast dich meiner erbarmt?

PAPAGENO:
What, you feel sorry for me?

ALTES WEIB:
Ja, mein Engel!

OLD WOMAN:
Yes, my angel!

PAPAGENO:
Na, das ist ein Glück!

PAPAGENO:
Am I lucky!

ALTES WEIB:
Und wenn du mir versprichst, mir ewig treu zu bleiben, dann sollst du sehen, wie zärtlich dein Weibchen dich lieben wird.

OLD WOMAN:
And if you promise to be true to me forever, then you'll see how tenderly your little wife will love you.

PAPAGENO:
Ei, du zärtliches Närrchen!

PAPAGENO:
Oh you tender little fool!

ALTES WEIB:
O. wie will ich dich umarmen, dich liebkosen, dich an mein Herz drücken!

OLD WOMAN:
Oh, how I'll embrace you, caress you, and press you to my heart!

PAPAGENO:
Auch ans Herz drücken?

PAPAGENO:
Even press me to your heart?

ALTES WEIB::
Komm, reich mir zum Pfand unsers Bundes deine Hand!

OLD WOMAN:
Come, give me your hand as a pledge of our union!

PAPAGENO::
Nur nicht so hastig, mein lieber Engel! So ein Bündnis braucht doch auch seine Überlegung.

PAPAGENO:
Not so fast, my dear angel! After all, such a union needs some consideration.

ALTES WEIB:
Papageno, ich rate dir, zaudre nicht! -
Deine Hand, oder du bist auf immer hier
eingekerkert.

PAPAGENO:
Eingekerkert?

ALTES WEIB:
Wasser und Brot wird deine tägliche Kost
sein. Ohne Freund, ohne Freundin mußt du
leben, und der Welt auf immer entsagen.

PAPAGENO:
Wasser trinken? Der Welt entsagen? Nein,
da will ich doch lieber eine Alte nehmen,
als gar keine. Also gut, da hast du meine
Hand mit der Versicherung, daß ich dir
immer getreu bleibe.
...olang ich keine Schönere sehe.

ALTES WEIB:
Das schwörst du?

PAPAGENO:
Ja, das schwör' ich!

OLD WOMAN:
Papageno, I advise you not to hesitate. Give
me your hand or you will be imprisoned
here forever.

PAPAGENO:
Imprisoned?

OLD WOMAN:
Bread and water will be your daily diet. You
must live without friends or sweetheart, and
renounce the world forever.

PAPAGENO:
I have to drink water and renounce the
world? No, then I prefer to have an old
woman than none at all. All right. Here is
my hand with my promise to be true to you
forever. *(aside)*
...as long as I don't see a prettier one.

OLD WOMAN:
Do you swear to that?

PAPAGENO:
Yes, I swear to it!

The Old Woman transforms into a young woman, dressed like Papageno.

Papagena! Papagena!

As he attempts to embrace her, the Priest comes and takes her by the hand.

SPRECHER:
Fort mit dir, junges Weib! Er ist deiner noch
nicht würdig!
Zurück sage ich.

PAPAGENO:
Soll ich zurückziehe, soll die Erde mich
verschlingen. O ihr Götter!

SPEAKER:
Away with you, young woman! He is not
yet worthy of you! *(to Papageno)*
I'm telling you to go back!

PAPAGENO:
Before I go back, the earth will swallow me
up. Oh you gods!

As the Speaker takes Papagena away, Papageno sinks into the earth.

The Three Youths arrive.

Andante
THREE YOUTHS

Bald prangt, den Morgen zu verkünden, die Sonn auf gold - ner Bahn.

DREI KNABEN:
Bald prangt, den Morgen zu verkünden,
die Sonn auf goldner Bahn.
Bald soll der Aberglaube schwinden.
Bald siegt der weise Mann.
O holde Ruhe, steig' hernieder,
kehr' in der Menschen Herzen wieder;
dann ist die Erd' ein Himmelreich,
ind Sterbliche den Göttern gleich.

THE THREE YOUTHS:
Soon the sun will rise to banish the night,
and beam its brilliance on the earth.
Soon all superstition will vanish.
Soon the wise man will be victorious.
Oh heavenly quiet, now descend,
and return to the heart of man.
Then the earth will be as heaven,
and mortals divine.

ERSTER KNABE:
Doch seht, Verzweiflung quält Paminen!

FIRST YOUTH:
But look, Pamina is suffering from doubt!

ZWEITER, DRITTER KNABE:
Wo ist sie denn?

SECOND AND THIRD YOUTH:
Where is she?

ERSTER KNABE:
Sie ist von Sinnen!

FIRST YOUTH:
She is out of her mind!

DREI KNABEN:
Sie quält verschmähter Liebe Leiden. Laßt
uns der Armen Trost bereiten!
Fürwahr, ihr Schicksal geht uns nah!
O wäre nur ihr Jüngling da!
Sie kommt, laßt uns beiseite gehn,
Damit wir, was sie mache, sehn.

THE THREE YOUTHS:
She suffers pangs of scorned love. Let our
embrace console her! Her fate has greatly
moved us! Oh if only her young man
would be here! Oh here she comes.
Let's move aside so we can observe her
better and prevent a fatal mistake.

*The Three Youths step aside. Pamina rushes in half insane,
holding the dagger given her by the Queen.*

PAMINA:
Du also bist mein Bräutigam?
Durch dich vollend' ich meinen Gram.

PAMINA: *(addressing her dagger)*
So you are my bridegroom?
Through you my grief will be ended!

DREI KNABEN:
Welch dunkle Worte sprach sie da?
Die Arme ist dem Wahnsinn nah.

PAMINA:
Geduld, mein Trauter, ich bin dein;
bald werden wir vermählet sein.

DREI KNABEN:
Wahnsinn tobt ihr im Gehirne;
selbstmord steht auf ihrer Stirne.

Holdes Mädchen, sieh uns an!

PAMINA:
Sterben will ich, weil der Mann,
Den ich nimmermehr kann hassen,
Sein Traute kann verlassen.

Dies gab meine Mutter mir.

DREI KNABEN:
Selbstmord strafet Gott an dir!

PAMINA:
Lieber durch dies Eisen sterben,
als durch Liebesgram verderben!
Mutter, durch dich leide ich,
und dein Fluch verfolget mich!

DREI KNABEN:
Mädchen, willst du mit uns gehn?

PAMINA:
Ha, des Jammers Maß ist voll!
Falscher Jüngling, lebe wohl!
Sieh, Pamina, ach! Stirbt durch dich,
dieses Eisen töte mich!

DREI KNABEN:

Ha, Unglückliche, halt ein! Sollte dies dein
Jüngling sehen, Würde er vor Gram
vergehen; Denn er liebet dich allein.

THE YOUTHS: *(aside)*
Oh, what sinister words did she say?
The poor soul is near madness!

PAMINA:
Patience, my beloved, I am yours. Soon we
will be united.

THE YOUTHS: *(draw nearer)*
Madness lurks in her mind.
She's contemplating suicide.
(To Pamina)
Lovely maiden, listen to us!

PAMINA:
Since I cannot hate the man I love,
and he has forsaken me,
I want to die.
(pointing to the dagger)
This, my mother gave to me.

THE THREE YOUTHS:
God will punish you if you commit suicide!

PAMINA:
I prefer to die by this dagger than to perish
as a grieving lover!
Mother, I suffer because of you, and your
curse that pursues me!

THE THREE YOUTHS:
Girl, do you want to come with us?

PAMINA:
Ah, my suffering is too much!
Faithless lover, farewell!
Look, Pamina dies because of you.
May this dagger kill me!

(She tries to stab herself)

THE THREE YOUTHS:
(snatching the dagger from her)
Stop, unhappy one! If your lover would see
this, he would die from sorrow, for you are
his only love.

PAMINA:
Was? Er fühlte Gegenliebe, und verbarg
mir seine Triebe, Wandte sein Gesicht vor
mir? Warum sprach er nicht mit mir?

DREI KNABEN::
Dieses müßen wir verschweigen, doch wir
wollen dir ihn zeigen! Und du wirst mit
Staunen sehn, daß er dir sein Herz geweiht,
und den Tod für dich nicht scheut. Komm,
wir wollen zu ihm gehen.

PAMINA:
Führt mich hin, ich möcht' ihn seh'n!

ALLE:
Zwei Herzen, die von Liebe brennen,
Kann Menschenohnmacht niemals trennen.
Verloren ist der Feinde Müh',
Die Götter selbst schützen sie.

PAMINA: *(recovering herself)*
What? He loves me, and concealed his
feelings for me and turned his face away?
Why didn't he speak to me?

THE THREE YOUTHS:
This, we're not allowed to tell you, but we
will show him to you! You will be amazed
at how much he loves you, and that he
would sacrifice his life for you. Come, let's
go to him!

PAMINA:
Take me to him, I'd love to see him!

ALL:
Two hearts that are burning with such true
love, humans can never separate.
The efforts of the enemy are in vain, for the
gods are protecting them from harm.

(All leave)

ACT II - Scene 7

*Rugged cliffs in the mountains at twilight.
There is a roaring stream, and a brightly glowing fire.*

DIE ZWEI GEHARNISCHTEN::
Der, welcher wandert diese Straße voll
Beschwerden, wird rein durch Feuer,
Wasser, Luft und Erden; wenn er des
Todes Schrecken überwinden kann, schwingt
er sich aus der Erde himmelan.Erleuchtet
wird er dann im Stande sein, sich den
Mysterien der Isis ganz zu weih'n.

TWO MEN IN ARMOR:
He who pursues this path full of dangers,
becomes purified by fire, water, air and
earth.
If he can overcome the fear of death, he
will rise to heaven. Thus purified, he then
will be able to devote himself completely to
Isis's mysteries.

TAMINO:
Mich schreckt kein Tod, als Mann zu handeln, den Weg der Tugend fortzuwandeln. Schließt mir die Schreckenspforten auf, ich wage froh den kühnen Lauf.

TAMINO:
I'm not afraid of death. Even death will not prevent me from acting as a man, and from walking the path of virtue. Open up the dreadful gates, and I'll gladly risk the dangers!

PAMINA:
Tamino, halt! Ich muß dich sehn.

PAMINA: *(from within)*
Tamino, stop! I must see you!

TAMINO:
Was hör ich? Paminens Stimme?

TAMINO:
What do I hear? Pamina's voice?

DIE GEHARNISCHTEN::
Ja, ja, das ist Paminens Stimme.

MEN:
Yes, yes, that is Pamina's voice.

ALLE:
Wohl mir/dir, nun kann sie mit mir/dir geh'n, nun trennet uns/euch kein Schicksal mehr, wenn auch der Tod beschieden wär!

ALL:
Fortunate me/you, now she can come with me/you. Destiny will no longer separate us/you, even in death!

TAMINO:
Ist mir erlaubt, mit ihr zu sprechen?

TAMINO:
Am I allowed to speak to her?

DIE GEHARNISCHTEN::
Dir ist erlaubt, mit ihr zu sprechen.

MEN:
You are allowed to speak to her.

ALLE:
Welch Glück, wenn wir uns/euch wiederseh'n. Froh Hand in Hand in Tempel geh'n! Ein Weib, das Nacht und Tod nicht scheut, ist würdig und wird eingeweiht.

ALL:
What joy when we will see you/each other again. Enter the temple joyfully, hand in hand. A wife unafraid of night and death, deserves to be ordained.

Priests bring in Pamina, and Pamina and Tamino embrace.

PAMINA:
Tamino mein! O welch ein Glück!

PAMINA:
My dear Tamino! What happiness this is!

TAMINO:
Pamina mein! O welch ein Glück!

Hier sind die Schreckenspforten,
Die Not und Tod mir dräu'n.

TAMINO:
My dear Pamina! What happiness this is!
(He points to both mountain caverns)
Here are the gates of horror that threaten me with danger and death.

PAMINA:
Ich werde aller Orten an deiner Seite sein;
Ich selbsten führe dich, die Liebe leitet mich!

Sie mag den Weg mit Rosen streun, weil
Rosen stets bei Dornen sein. Spiel du die
Zauberflöte an; Sie schütze uns auf uns'rer
Bahn.
Es schnitt in einer Zauberstunde. Mein Vater
sie aus tiefstem Grunde Der tausendjähr'gen
Eiche aus, Bei Blitz und Donner, Sturm und
Braus. Nun komm und spiel' die Flöte an, Sie
leite uns auf grauser Bahn.

TAMINO, PAMINA:
Wir wandeln (Ihr wandelt) durch des Tones
Macht Froh durch des Todes düstre Nacht.

PAMINA:
I will always be by your side. I myself will
lead you, for I am guided by love.

(Pamina takes Tamino by the hand)
Although our path will be strewn with
thorny roses, our love will prevail. Now
you'll play your magic flute. It will protect
us on our way.
My father used his magical powers to
fashion it himself from a thousand-year old
oak tree during thunder, lightning, storm
and gale. Now play your magic flute, for it
will protect us on our way.

TAMINO, PAMINA:
With the flute's power, we wander (you
wander) happily through death's darkness.

Tamino and Pamina pass through the fiery cave while he plays the flute.
As soon as they emerge from the ordeal of fire, they embrace.

PAMINA, TAMINO:
Wir wandelten durch Feuersgluten,
Bekämpften mutig die Gefahr.

Dein Ton sei Schutz in Wasserfluten,
So wie er es im Feuer war.

PAMINA, TAMINO:
We wandered through the flames, and
bravely overcame the dangers.
(to the flute)
May your tones protect us in the flood of
waters, as they did in the fires.

Tamino and Pamina proceed into the cave of water,
and emerge shortly thereafter.

PAMINA, TAMINO:
Ihr Götter, welch ein Augenblick!
Gewähret ist uns Isis' Glück!

CHOR: :
Triumph! Triumph! Du edles Paar!
Besieget hast du die Gefahr!
Der Isis Weihe ist nun dein!
Kommt, tretet in den Tempel ein!

PAMINA, TAMINO:
Oh gods, what a glorious sight!
The joy of Isis is upon us!

CHORUS OF PRIESTS:
Triumph! Triumph! You noble pair!
You have overcome the danger!
You are now consecrated to Isis!
Come, enter the temple!

Tamino and Pamina enter the temple.

ACT II - Scene 8

Daylight. A small garden. Papageno appears with a rope wrapped around his waist.

PAPAGENO::
Papagena! Papagena! Papagena!
Weibchen! Täubchen! Meine Schöne!
Vergebens! Ach, sie ist verloren!
Ich bin zum Unglück schon geboren!
Ich plauderte, und das war schlecht,
und drum geschieht es mir schon recht!

Seit ich gekostet diesen Wein,
seit ich das schöne Weibchen sah,
so brennt's im Herzenskämmerlein,
so zwickt's hier, so zwickt's da.

Papagena! Herzensweibchen!
Papagena, liebes Täubchen!
Es ist umsonst, es ist vergebens!
Müde bin ich meines Lebens!
Sterben macht der Lieb' ein End',
wenn's im Herzen noch so brennt.

Diesen Baum da will ich zieren,
mir an ihm den Hals zuschnüren,
weil das Leben mir mißfällt;
gute Nacht, du falsche Welt.
Weil du böse an mir handelst,
mir kein schönes Kind zubandelst,
so ist's aus, so sterbe ich;
schöne Mädchen, denkt an mich.

Will sich eine um mich Armen,
Eh' ich hänge, noch erbarmen,
Nun, so laß ich's diesmal sein!
Rufet nur, ja oder nein.

Keine hört mich; alles stille!
Also ist es euer Wille?
Papageno, frisch hinauf!
Ende deinen Lebenslauf!

Nun, ich warte noch, es sei,
Bis man zählet: eins, zwei, drei.

PAPAGENO:
Papagena! Papagena! Papagena!
Little woman! Little dove! My beauty!
It's hopeless! Ah, I've lost her!
I was born to be miserable!
I talked, and that was wrong,
so it serves me right!.

Since I tasted that wine and saw that
beautiful little woman, there has been a
constant fire burning in my heart
that's torturing me day and night!

Papagena! Light of my life!
Papagena, darling little dove!
It's no use, it's all hopeless!
I'm tired of life!
Nothing is left for me but to die,
even though my heart is burning.

(He takes the rope)
I've chosen this tree to hang from,
since life is no longer worth living.
Farewell deceitful world since you treated
me so badly, and refused to grant me a
beautiful mate, all is over and I shall die.
Lovely girl, remember me.

In case someone wants to love or pity me
before I hang myself,
just call out to me, yes or no.

(Papageno looks around)
No one hears me, all is quiet!
Tell me then, is it your will?
Papageno, swing up high!
End your life!
(He looks around)
Well, I'll wait a while.
I'll count from one, two, three.

Eins!	*(He whistles)* One!
Zwei!	*(He looks around and whistles)* Two!
Drei!	*(He looks around and whistles)* Three!
Nun, wohlan, es bleibt dabei, weil mich nichts zurücke hält, Gute Nacht, du falsche Welt!	*(He looks around)* Well then, let it be! While nothing is stopping me, goodnight then you deceitful world!

As Papageno tries to hang himself, the Three Youths hurry in.

DREI KNABEN:
Halt ein, o Papageno! und sei klug,
man lebt nur einmal, dies sei dir genug!

THE THREE YOUTHS:
Stop Papageno, be smart! You only live once, and let that be enough for you!

PAPAGENO:
Ihr habt gut reden, habt gut scherzen;
doch brennt' es euch, wie mich im Herzen,
ihr würdet auch nach Mädchen gehn.

PAPAGENO:
It's easy for you to talk and joke. If your hearts would burn like mine, you would also chase young girls.

DREI KNABEN::
So lasse deine Glöckchen klingen,
dies wird dein Weibchen zu dir bringen.

THE THREE YOUTHS:
Then let your magic bells ring. They will bring your little woman to you.

PAPAGENO::
Ich Narr vergaß der Zauberdinge!
Erklinge, Glockenspiel, erklinge!
Ich muß mein liebes Mädchen seh'n.
Klinget, Glöckchen, klinget,
Schafft mein Mädchen her!
Klinget, Glöckchen, klinget!
Bringt mein Weibchen her.

PAPAGENO:
I'm such a fool, I forgot the magic thing!
Ring, bells, ring!
I must see my dear little girl.
Ring little bells, ring!
Bring my little girl!
Ring, bells, ring!
Bring my little girl to me!

He plays the glockenspiel, and then the Three Youths return with Papagena.

DREI KNABEN:
Nun, Papageno, sieh dich um!

THREE YOUTHS:
Now, Papageno, turn around!

The Three Youths leave. Papageno turns around, sees Papagena, and becomes dumbfounded.

PAPAGENO:
Pa-pa-pa-pa-pa-pa-Papagena!

PAPAGENA:
Pa-pa-pa-pa-pa-pa-Papageno!

BEIDE:
Pa-Pa-Pa-Pa-Pa-Papageno! Papagena!

PAPAGENO:
Bist du mir nun ganz gegeben?

PAPAGENA:
Nun, bin ich dir ganz gegeben!

PAPAGENO:
Nun, so sei mein liebes Weibchen!

PAPAGENA:
Nun, so sei mein Herzenstäubchen!

BEIDE:
Welche Freude wird das sein, wenn die Götter uns bedenken, unsrer liebe Kinder schenken, so liebe, kleine Kinderlein!

PAPAGENO::
Erst einen kleinen Papageno.

PAPAGENA:
Dann eine kleine Papagena.

PAPAGENO:
Dann wieder einen Papageno.

PAPAGENA:
Dann wieder eine Papagena-

BEIDE:
Papageno! Papagena!
Es ist das höchste der Gefühle,
wenn viele, viele Papageno/a,
der Eltern Segen werden sein.

PAPAGENO: *(dancing around her)*
Pa-Pa-Pa-Pa-Pa-Papagena!

PAPAGENA: *(dancing around him)*
Pa-Pa-Pa-Pa-Pa-Papageno!

BOTH:
Pa-Pa-Pa-Pa-Pa Papageno! Papagena!

PAPAGENO:
Are you really all mine now?

PAPAGENA:
Yes, I'm really all yours now!

PAPAGENO:
So then be my little wife!

PAPAGENA:
Now then be my little sweetheart!

BOTH:
What a joy it would be if the gods would bless us with children, very darling little children!

PAPAGENO:
First a little Papageno.

PAPAGENA:
Then a little Papagena.

PAPAGENO:
Then another Papageno.

PAPAGENA:
Then another Papagena.

BOTH:
Papagena! Papagena!
It would be the greatest feeling
if we would be blessed with many
Papagenos and Papagenas.

Both leave arm in arm.

ACT II - Scene 9

*Rugged cliffs. It is dark. Monostatos, the Queen,
and the Three Ladies appear with lighted torches.*

MONOSTATOS:
Nur stille, stille, stille,
bald dringen wir im Tempel ein.

ALLE::
Nur stille, stille, stille,
bald dringen wir im Tempel ein.

MONOSTATOS:
Doch, Fürstin, halte Wort!
Erfülle dein Kind muß meine Gattin sein.

KÖNIGIN:
Ich halte Wort; es ist mein Wille, mein Kind
soll deine Gattin sein.

DREI DAMEN:
Ihr Kind soll deine Gattin sein.

MONOSTATOS: *(near the Queen)*
All is quiet, quiet, quiet!
Soon we will enter the temple.

ALL THE LADIES:
All is quiet, quiet, quiet!
Soon we will enter the temple.

MONOSTATOS:
You, Queen, will keep your word,
your child must become my wife!

QUEEN:
I keep my word, I want my child to be your wife.

ALL THE LADIES:
Her child will be his wife.

The sounds of thunder and rushing water are heard.

MONOSTATOS:
Doch still, ich höre schrecklich Rauschen,
wie Donnerton und Wasserfall.

KÖNIGIN, DIE DAMEN:
Ja, fürchterlich ist dieses Rauschen,
Wie fernen Donners Widerhall!

MONOSTATOS:
Nun sind sie in des Tempels Hallen.

ALLE::
Dort wollen wir sie überfallen. Die
Frömmler tilgen von der Erd' mit
Feuerglut und mächt'gem Schwert.

DREI DAMEN, MONOSTATOS:
Dir, große Königin der Nacht,
sei uns'rer Rache Opfer gebracht.

MONOSTATOS:
Quiet! I hear a frightful roaring, like
thunder and a waterfall.

QUEEN AND LADIES:
Yes, this roaring is horrible, like the echo of
distant thunder!

MONOSTATOS:
Now they're assembling in the temple hall.

ALL:
We will overtake them there. We will
destroy them with sword and fire, and
remove those hypocrites from the earth.

LADIES AND MONOSTATOS:
To satisfy your vengeance, we will bring the
victims to you, great Queen of the Night.

Thunder, lightning, and storm.

ALLE::
Zerschmettert, zernichtet ist unsere Macht,
Wir alle gestürzt in ewige Nacht!

ALL:
Our power is destroyed and demolished,
and we'll be hurled into eternal darkness!

They all sink into the earth.

ACT II - Scene 10

*Temple of the Sun. Sarastro, Priests and Priestesses.
Tamino and Pamina stand before Sarastro.*

SARASTRO:
Die Strahlen der Sonne vertreiben die
Nacht, Zernichten der Heuchler
erschlichene Macht.

SARASTRO:
The sun's radiant glory has vanquished the
night, and has destroyed the deceiving
powers of the hypocrites.

CHOR::
Heil sei euch Geweihten!
Ihr dränget durch Nacht.
Dank sei dir, Osiris,
Dank dir, Isis, gebracht!
Es siegte die Stärke
Und krönet zum Lohn
Die Schönheit und Weisheit
Mit ewiger Kron'.

CHORUS OF PRIESTS:
Glory to the consecrated!
You have been guided through darkness,
thanks to Osiris,
and thanks to Isis.
The strong have conquered,
and as their reward,
they are crowned
with eternal beauty and wisdom.

Ende

THE END

Printed in Great Britain
by Amazon